THEIR
WAR

THEIR WAR

German Combat Photographs From the Archives of Signal

WILL FOWLER

MIKE ROSE

COMBINED PUBLISHING
Pennsylvania

PUBLISHER'S NOTE

The headquarters of Combined Publishing are located midway between Valley Forge and the Germantown battlefield, on the outskirts of Philadelphia. From its beginnings, our company has been steeped in the oldest traditions of American history and publishing. Our historic surroundings help maintain our focus on history and our books strive to uphold the standards of style, quality and durability first established by the earliest bookmakers of Germantown and Philadelphia so many years ago. Our famous monk-and-console logo reflects our commitment to the modern and yet historic enterprise of publishing.

We call ourselves Combined Publishing because we have always felt that our goals could only be achieved through a "combined" effort by authors, publishers and readers. We have always tried to maintain maximum communication between these three key players in the reading experience.

We are always interested in hearing from prospective authors about new books in our field. We also like to hear from our readers and invite you to contact us at our offices in Pennsylvania with any questions, comments or suggestions, or if you have difficulty finding our books at a local bookseller.

Combined Publishing

P.O. Box 307
Conshohocken, PA 19428

Text and captions written by Will Fowler.

Designed and developed by Mike Rose.

Front cover photo by Bugle Studios.

Picture Credits

All Photograghs and maps in THEIR WAR are derived from *Signal* or *Die Wehrmacht*, except for:
Pg 1 PC, Pg 6 – Pg 7 PC, Pg 8 (l) PC, Pg 9 PC, Pg 10 – Pg 12 PC, Pg 14 PC, Pg 19 PC, Pg 20 PC, Pg 22 – Pg 23 PC, Pg 25 PC, Pg 29 PC, Pg 30 (tp) PC, Pg 33 – Pg 35 PC, Pg 38 PC, Pg 39 (tp and btm rt) PC, Pg 40 – Pg 41 PC, Pg 42 (tp and rt) PC, Pg 46 (tp) PC, Pg 49 (tp) PC, Pg 51 (tp and lt) PC, Pg 52 (l) PC, Pg 53 PC, Pg 55 – Pg 56 PC, Pg 59 PC, Pg 63 (btm) PC, Pg 64 (tp) PC, Pg 67 (btm) PC, Pg 70 PC, Pg 71 (btm lt) PC, Pg 72 – 73 PC, Pg 90 (tp) US National Archives (btm) PC, Pg 95 (btm) PC, Pg 98 PC, Pg 99 (tp) PC, Pg 100 (btm) PC, Pg 101 PC, Pg 103 PC, Pg 113 PC, Pg 119 (btm) PC, Pg 121 (tp) PC, Pg 123 (lt) PC, Pg 124 (mdle) PC, Pg 129 PC, Pg 131 (tp rt) PC, Pg 132 PC, Pg 133 (btm) PC, Pg 135 (btm) PC, Pg 136 (btm lt) PC, Pg 138 (btm rt) PC, Pg 140 (rt) PC, Pg 142 (btm lt) PC, Pg 145 PC, Pg 147 (btm) Sovfoto, Pg 149 (mdle and btm) PC, Pg 154 (tp) US National Archives (lt) PC, Pg 155 (tp and lt) US National Archives, Pg 156 (tp lt and btm) US National Archives (tp rt) PC, Pg 157 US National Archives, Pg 158 (tp lt and rt) PC, Pg 159 PC.
(Pg = Page, PC = Private Collection, tp = top, rt = right, lt = left, btm = bottom, mdl = middle)

ISBN 1-58097-040-0

Printed in the United States of America

CONTENTS

INTRODUCTION

An honor guard from the *Leibstandarte SS Adolf Hitler* awaits a dignitary in Berlin in the late 1930s.

Hitler ascends to the podium past massed SA banners at a rally at Bückeberg in 1934.

*S*ignal, the stylish German propaganda newsmagazine that at the height of its circulation published in twenty languages, lasted for exactly five years. Yet despite this short life, its impact and images remain with us today. Color photographs of German and Axis troops and their leaders make the events of nearly sixty years ago powerfully vivid.

Signal modeled itself on magazines like the British *Picture Post* and American *Life* and *National Geographic*. The magazine celebrated German victories and the Nazi's *Neuordnung*—New Order in Europe with lavish use of color and black and white photography, cartoons, maps, and diagrams. In a world in which television was barely in its infancy and computers and the web the stuff of science fiction, the most effective way to reach a mass audience, other than radio, was in print through large format newsmagazines.

The driving force behind the propaganda war waged by Nazi Germany was Dr. Paul Joseph Goebbels. Goebbels was the only intellectual in the senior hierarchy of the Nazi Party and had worked in journalism before he joined the Nazi Party at the age of 25 in 1922. He had studied American journalism and advertising techniques and used these skills when in 1933 he was made *Reichsminister für Volkserklärung und Propaganda*—Reich Minister for Public Enlightenment and Propaganda.

The stated editorial policy behind *Signal* was to advertise National Socialist Germany, support the country's allies with it, gain "the trust and willingness to work of the population in the occupied territories," and influence neutral states in Europe and South America toward a "pro-German and anti-inimical opinion."

Unlike the domestic press in Germany, it avoided anti-Semitic propaganda; though

following the invasion of the USSR it contrasted idealized German soldiers with the lower orders of Slavs and Central Asians they were conquering.

At one stage the fortnightly magazine circulated in Belgium, Bohemia and Moravia, Bulgaria, Croatia, Denmark, Estonia, Finland, France, Greece, Hungary, Iran, Italy, Luxembourg, the Netherlands, Norway, Portugal, Romania, Sweden, Switzerland, Serbia, Slovakia, Spain, Turkey, and an English language version was even produced for the United States and the Occupied Channel Islands. Each version was priced in the national currency, so American readers could buy their *Signal* for 10 cents.

The name for the magazine was chosen because "signal" was a word that was universal throughout Europe. The multilingual production of *Signal* reflects the arrogant confidence of the Third Reich—even before they had conquered France and Belgium they were producing a French language version. However after 1943 *Signal* presented a version of Nazi Germany that was increasingly at variance with the reality of a continent suffering shortages and under constant air attack. The Germany shown in *Signal* was a land untroubled by war where the harvest was gathered in, artists and craftsmen thrived, and the war was at a safe distance. Advertisements for luxury goods like perfume and cosmetics appear alongside those promoting military equipment.

While half of the color in the magazine was devoted to news stories, half was retained for domestic, artistic, or pin up photographs. Pictures of fair-haired, bikini-clad girls on Germany's Baltic beaches were put up in bunkers and barracks by both German and Allied troops. The highly acclaimed Australian journalist and war correspondent Alan Moorehead had a *Signal* pin up that traveled with him and once it was on the wall of even the most dilapidated accommodation, the building became "home."

The first edition of *Signal*, produced under the authority of the Wehrmacht Propaganda Department of the *Oberkommando der Wehrmacht* (OKW), came out in April 1940 and the last appeared on April 13, 1945. It was a fortnightly supplement of the weekly illustrated publication the *Berliner Illustrierte Zeitung* or BI and so in effect became the world's first newspaper color

The *Führer* signs copies of *Mein Kampf* as Dr. Goebbels looks on. *Signal* was the brainchild of Dr. Joseph Goebbels, the Nazi master of propaganda.

A 2-cm light Flak gun during prewar maneuvers at the Reich Party Day at Nurenberg in 1935.

A classic propaganda photograph of German soldiers in the early M1915 helmet emphasises the Nazi *Wehrmachtadler* insignia. The *Reichswehr* in 1933 had become the *Wehrmacht*—the military instrument of the Third Reich.

supplement. Initially magazines were identified by month and year, but by 1944 it had become expedient to simple give each magazine a number.

In 1943 at almost the apogee of Nazi power, its total circulation was about two and a half million with about a fifth published in German and 800,000 in French. Its editor in chief until September 1941 was Harald Lechenberg; Heinz von Medefind acted in his place until spring of 1942; then Wilhelm Reetz held the position until the February 1945 issue.

In the last months of Nazi Germany the post went to Giselher Wirsing who had been *de facto* editor in chief since May 1943. Wirsing was a committed Nazi who had joined the *Shutzstaffel*—SS in 1933 and as a *Sturmbannführer* (Major) worked intermittently in the National Socialist Institute for Research on the Jewish Question.

After the war Wirsing became editor in chief of the conservative weekly newspaper *Christ und Welt* (*The Christian and the World 1954–1970*). He died in Stuttgart in 1975.

It has now become difficult to track down copies of *Signal*, and indeed many that exist are in poor condition. Many of the unique images collected in this book are thus the products of research over several years in Great Britain and Europe.

Some events in the war in Europe and Russia were not covered by *Signal* photographers, either because the magazine had not been set up, or because like the Allied preparations for D Day they were shrouded in secrecy and took place miles behind the enemy front lines.

For a more complete history of the war some pictures from Allied sources or German publications like the official German Army magazine *Die Wehrmacht* have been included. These images combine together to present a different picture of World War II as seen through German eyes—Their War.

An NCO of the Army press unit, the *Propagandakompanien (PK)* at work in 1940 on news reports in France. The *PK* teams provided *Signal* with superb photographs.

THE YEARS OF VICTORY
1939–1943

"I have decided, without loss of time, to go over to the offensive. Any further delay will not only entail the end of Belgian and perhaps Dutch neutrality, to the advantage of the Allies, but it will increasingly strengthen the military power of the enemy, reduce the confidence of the neutral nations in Germany's final victory, and make it more difficult to bring Italy as a full ally into the war."

—Adolf Hitler *October 9,*

POLAND, SCANDINAVIA AND THE LOW COUNTRIES

▲ The *Berliner Illustrierte Zeitung*, the popular illustrated newspaper known to many of its readers "B I," was where *Signal* first appeared as a color supplement.

▶ The *Führer* surveys his conquests; Hitler in the front line in Poland in 1939 observes through periscopic artillery binoculars commonly known to German gunners as "donkey's ears."

FOR THE EDITOR AND STAFF OF *Signal* it could be said that World War II began ahead of the publication schedule. The concept of the magazine was still in the planning stages when at dawn on September 1, 1939, in an operation code-named *Fall Weiss* (Case White), four German armies punched across Poland's borders. In great curving thrusts they cut off the Polish armies deployed along the western frontier.

The first issue of the German propaganda magazine was not published until nearly seven months later and so the opening events of World War II, including Poland and operations in Denmark and Norway, were covered in retrospective articles that appeared in the spring of 1940.

For the German public and a disbelieving world the pretext for the German attack on Poland in 1939 were aggressive Polish border incursions. These were in reality faked incidents that included the notorious Gleiwitz Raid, the fabricated attack on a radio station on the German Polish border by "Polish troops."

The attack at 1930 on August 31, 1939, was undertaken by SS men in Polish uniforms commanded by the SD officer Alfred Helmut Naujocks. They beat up the radio station staff, made a

▲ A Grenadier hurls a StiGr 24 stick grenade. It weighed 595 grams and the fuse to the TNT filling gave a 4 to 5 second delay.

◀ A German MG 34 machine gun crew take up a fire position on top of a Polish road block. The MG 34 had a maximum range of 2,000 meters, a cyclic rate of 800 – 900 rounds per minute, and fired from a 75-round saddle drum magazine or 50-round non-disintegrating belts.

brief broadcast urging Poland to attack Germany, and fled, leaving behind as evidence the body of one of their group. This corpse was that of an inmate of a concentration camp selected as part of an operation called *"Canned Goods"* and shot on site by the raiders.

For France and Great Britain the attack on Poland, whose security they had guaranteed, was the fatal move. They were committed to declaring war—Great Britain at 11:00 a.m. and France at 5:00 p.m. on September 3, 1939.

The indicators of Hitler's voracious territorial ambitions and the inevitability of war had culminated in the Munich Agreement, signed on September 29–30, 1938, between Germany, Italy, France, and Britain. It ceded the German-speaking Sudetenland of western Czechoslovakia to Germany. In August, Hitler had mobilized his army and threatened to attack the Czechs. Chamberlain, the British, and Daladier, the French prime minister, had a series of meetings in which they were pressured by Hitler and in turn pressed the Czechs. At Munich, a modified version of Hitler's demands was deemed acceptable to the Anglo French leaders. This appeasement allowed Hitler to dominate his generals, who believed that France and Britain would call the Führer's bluff and go to war. The French and British leaders were gleefully portrayed by Nazi propaganda as weak and vacillating.

The Munich Agreement is often seen as the low point of the

▼ A soldier takes aim with the 7.92 mm Karabiner Kar 98 K, the standard rifle that had a maximum effective range of 800 meters.

◄ In a locked and shuttered north Polish town German soldiers pry open a window. Their casual manner suggests that this is a search for loot or possibly Polish soldiers evading capture.

▶ German soldiers come under sniper fire in the ruins of Warsaw. Judging by their light order of equipment they are "mopping up" after the street fighting. The city finally fell on September 27, 1939, with the major center of Polish resistance.

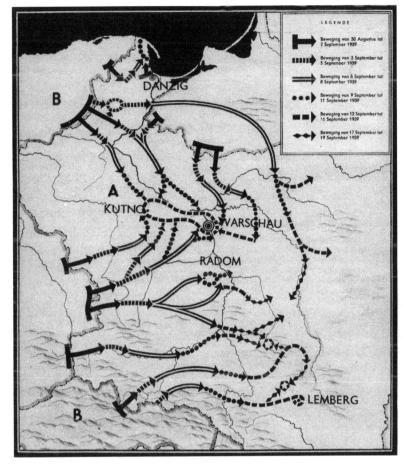

▶ A map from *Signal* showing the thrust lines of the German panzer divisions that tore Poland apart in September 1939.

policy of appeasement, but it was also an awakening in the West to the threat posed by Nazi Germany. It bought time for Britain and France who began to accelerate re-armament and in conjunction with Poland work began on breaking the German Enigma code machines.

The Enigma was a highly sophisticated mechanical encryption system used in radio transmissions that the Germans firmly believed was completely secure. The secrecy for the project was at such a high level that it was classified "Ultra Secret" and became known as ULTRA.

ULTRA was still in its infancy in autumn 1939 and could not save Poland. In four weeks the invading German armies, consisting of the 3rd and 4th Armies of Army Group North under General Fedor von Bock, and the 8th, 10th, and 14th Armies of Army Group South under General Gerd von Rundstedt, had defeated the Poles. However this collapse was accelerated by the invasion of eastern Poland by the Red Army on September 17.

◀ Hitler takes the salute at the victory parade in Warsaw. He wears the fine grain gray-green leather greatcoat that could be privately purchased by officers. His Army *Reichsadler* sleeve insignia is unique.

▶ An MG 34 crew dash past the gutted remains of a Norwegian house in the late winter of 1940. They carry assault order equipment on their belts including entrenching tool, bayonet, and respirator in its ribbed metal container.

▶ In the victory parade in Warsaw, German troops have not adopted the dramatic, but exhausting "parade march" widely known as the "goose step." Germany felt it had good reason to celebrate having defeated a major nation in about a month with only 8,082 killed.

A major tenet of National Socialism had been a loathing of Communism. In his speeches in the 1930s, Hitler had rolled anti-Semitism and hatred of "Bolshevism" into ranting outbursts that had enraptured his audiences. It caused shock and surprise therefore to Communists, Nazis, and conservative Germans alike when on August 20, 1939, Hitler telegrammed Stalin to urge an agreement because of the "worsening situation in Poland."

On August 23, 1939, the Russo-German Pact between Nazi Germany and Communist Russia was signed in Moscow by the German Foreign Minister von Ribbentrop and Soviet Minister Molotov. Hitler in a piece of brutal pragmatism had ensured that the USSR would not intervene to support the Poles.

Warsaw capitulated on September 27 and the last vestige of resistance ended by October 5. The campaign had cost the Germans 8,082 killed, 27,278 wounded, and 5,029 missing. The Poles lost 70,000 killed and 130,000 wounded.

It was the first demonstration of the tactics of deep penetration by a combination of fast moving armored columns supported by Ju 87 Stuka dive-bombers.

To describe this new way of war an Italian journalist gave it the nickname *Blitzkrieg*—Lightning War.

The Russo German Pact allowed the Germans to carve Poland in half with the USSR and also gave the Soviet giant a free hand in the Baltic.

On November 30, 1939, the USSR invaded Finland. The Soviet leader Joseph Stalin had already established with the Nazi foreign minister Joachim von Ribbentrop that the Baltic States of Latvia, Lithuania, and Estonia were in the Soviet sphere of influence. In October 1939 a "mutual assistance pact" was agreed between the USSR and Latvia. In June 1940, while the world watched the German invasion of the West, the USSR effortlessly gathered up the three tiny states.

▲ German troops in Norway. The man wearing the M1915 helmet is armed with a 9 mm MP 34 submachine gun. The weapon, widely known as a *Steyr-Solothurn,* was one of many taken from Austrian police and army stocks in 1938.

Finland however was a different customer. Stalin saw the close proximity of the Finnish border to Leningrad, the second city of the USSR, as a threat. He offered a mutual assistance treaty and demanded that Finland cede areas of the Karelian Isthmus close to Leningrad. Finland refused on both counts and the USSR invaded. In that bitter winter, 15 Finnish divisions inflicted a heavy defeat on 45 Soviet divisions.

In February 1940, the Allied War Council decided to send a 50,000 strong expeditionary force to support Finland. As it was being assembled the Soviets committed more forces to the attack and broke through the fortified belt known as the Mannerheim line. Finland was forced to sign a treaty on March 15, 1940, in which she ceded the city of Viborg, the Karelian Isthmus, and other territory.

In 1940 Norway was neutral and German cargo ships used her ice-free port of Narvik to collect high-grade Swedish iron ore for the war industries of the Ruhr. The British considered mining the coastal waters to disrupt this traffic and even a landing at Narvik. Hitler forestalled these plans with Operation *Weserübung* (Weser Exercise), a name that sounded as if the army was holding a simple river crossing exercise in Germany.

▼ Hunched behind a PzKpfw I tank, German soldiers advance cautiously down a Norwegian road. They have strapped blankets around the mess tins attached to the Y straps of their load carrying equipment.

▲ As the PzKpfw I Ausf A starts to accelerate the soldiers run to keep up with it. The tank was armed with twin MG 34s with 3,125 rounds and had a crew of two.

▼ This three dimensional diagram from *Signal* shows Operation *Weserübung*, the land, sea and air assault on Denmark and Norway in 1940.

▶ At Narvik, a German paratrooper waves the Swastika as an air identification marker for a Junkers Ju 52. The Ju 52 had a crew of two or three, and could carry 12 parachutists or 17 men. Its distinctive shape would appear regularly in the pages of *Signal*.

▲ The harbor at Narvik in April 1940 clogged with sunk or burning transports and warships. In the two sea battles at Narvik on April 9, and April 13, 1940, the Royal Navy reduced the German navy (*Kriegsmarine*) destroyer strength by half.

Weserübung was quite simply the invasion of Denmark and Norway. At 0415 on April 9, 1940, two German motorized brigade groups crossed the border. Assisted by parachute and airlanding attacks on the airfields at Aalborg in north Jutland and the key bridges between the islands, they quickly overwhelmed the country. The Danes were obliged to accept the presence of the invaders, however the government remained in place and the courts and police remained under Danish control. King Frederik IX, who remained in the country, provided a focus for loyalty and until August 1943 the government retained some independence.

Denmark was effectively a stepping stone to the Germans for the invasion of Norway. The German forces commanded by Colonel General Niklaus von Falkenhorst were divided into five groups. Group I landed at Narvik in the north, Group II at Trondheim, Group III at Bergen, Group IV at Kristiansand, and Group V aimed at Oslo, the Norwegian capital, where they would be assisted by airborne forces.

Norway, like Finland, was not a nation to accept invaders and, though her forces were not fully mobilized, they put up a tough and very creditable resistance. The modern 13,000-ton heavy cruiser KMS *Blücher* carrying troops and equipment up an Oslo fjord was sunk in Drôbak fjord by torpedoes fired from the Norwegian coastal fort at Kaholm. *Signal* would later feature the operation in dramatic three dimensional maps that even showed the loss of the *Blücher*. Germany was after all at war and losses are inevitable—an acceptable price for final victory.

▲ German *Fallschirmjäger* (paratroops) of the 1st Battalion of the 1st Parachute Regiment (FJR 1) forming up at Bjornfell above Narvik. The officer addressing these airborne reinforcements wears service dress that shows his yellow *Luftwaffe* collar patches. The men wear the distinctive rimless helmet with its double chin strap. The man on the left of the left-hand picture wears the distinctive paratroops ammunition bandoleer.

▲ A Rating from one of the sunken German destroyers at Narvik dressed in a captured Norwegian army tunic and leather equipment. Sailors became "marines" during the battle for Narvik, fighting as ground troops.

▲ A German motorcycle combination waits at a coastal ferry in Narvik. The rider wears the issue rubberized coat, the *Shutzmantel für Kraft Radfahrer*, a garment that could be buttoned around the wearer's legs to give added protection against rain and mud. The vehicle is a 750-cc *Kraftrad BMW R75 mit Seitenwagen* (with sidecar) that had a maximum road speed of 92 kmh.

The delays imposed on the task force at Oslo gave King Haakon VII and the Norwegian royal family enough time to escape via Andalsnes to Great Britain. Earlier the king had refused to accept a government headed by the Norwegian Nazi Vidkun Quisling, stating that he would rather abdicate than endorse the Norwegian traitor.

The German forces that landed at Oslo pushed inland and linked up with Group II and III. Southern Norway passed under German control by April 16. In the north the French, Polish, and British forces that had originally been intended for Finland were landed at Andalsnes, Namsos, and Narvik.

The German forces had landed at Narvik but in two naval actions the Royal Navy attacked warships and cargo ships on April 9 and April 13, 1940. The two actions accounted for nine destroyers and seven transports including the German ammunition ship *Rauenfels* that blew up. This trapped the mixed German

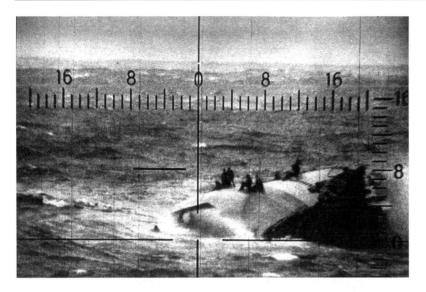

◀ The surviving crew of the destroyer HMS *Glowworm*, seen through the graticule of the main armament of the KMS *Admiral Hipper,* cling to the hull after it had rammed the German cruiser off the Norwegian coast on April 8. *Signal* ran a special feature on the heroic but doomed action.

army and naval forces ashore and it was only the developments in France and the Low Countries that forced the Allies to evacuate Narvik on May 31 and cheated them of victory.

On April 8 the men of the 13,900-ton heavy cruiser KMS *Admiral Hipper* encountered the 1,345-ton destroyer HMS *Glowworm* that had become detached from escorting the battle cruiser HMS *Renown* off Norway. In a short but heroic action, the German sailors watched as under heavy fire the *Glowworm*

▼ German gunners man a captured Norwegian coastal artillery position. Despite a partial mobilization Norwegian forces fought bravely and the heavy cruiser KMS *Blücher,* picked out by searchlights at dawn on April 9, 1940, was sunk by torpedoes from a coastal battery as she entered Oslo fjord.

▲ German infantry from Group V ride in an open topped freight car as they push northward from Oslo to link up with Group II that had landed at Trondheim. The two groups met at Dragset on April 29.

closed the range with the cruiser and rammed it before finally sinking. The damaged *Admiral Hipper* was forced to return to Germany but only one officer and 30 members of the crew of *Glowworm* survived. Dramatic photographs taken from the *Admiral Hipper* appeared in *Signal*, an indisputable record of the heroism of the captain and crew of the British destroyer.

The conquest of Denmark and Norway cost the Germans 5,500 men, over 200 aircraft, and a number of their most modern warships. The depletion of the Kriegsmarine would be a significant factor in plans for the invasion of Britain that were only considered after the fall of France in June 1940.

As the land battle for Narvik was drawing to a close a huge onslaught was about to explode across Western Europe. The anodyne code name for the invasion of Belgium, Holland, and France was *Fall Gelb* (Case Yellow).

▼ *Gebirgsjäger* (mountain troops) in a captured Norwegian fishing boat scan the skies for RAF aircraft. The MG 34 machine gun is on the Dreifuss 34 high angle AA stand. For added stability ammunition boxes were often slung on the mount.

▲ A train stops and troops scramble off to secure the high ground as it passes through a wooded cutting. Norway's mountains funneled road and rail communications through gorges and gullies.

▶ A 2 cm Flak 30 AA gun covering the approaches to a fjord. The Flak 30 weighed 483 kg in action, had an elevation of -120° to + 90°, and a maximum vertical range of 2,134 meters.

▲ Medium pneumatic boats linked as an infantry assault bridge. There were no limits on the length of a bridge of this configuration but it was unstable in currents above two knots. The boat was 5.5 meters long, weighed 150 kg and could carry seven men.

The original plan proposed for the invasion of France was a variant of the Schlieffen Plan. This had been devised by the Prussian chief of the general staff, General Count Alfred von Schlieffen, at the turn of the century. In a modified form it was put into action in August 1914 at the beginning of World War I, but halted at the battle of the Marne. The original idea required German forces to invade neutral Belgium and in a great swinging maneuver close on Paris from the northwest.

The trouble with the Schlieffen Plan was that it was no secret and the French and British now agreed with the Belgians that if

▶ A three-meter-long, small pneumatic boat overcrowded with four men attempts to cross a small river.

▲ A German Pioneer armed with a *Flammenwerfer* 35 flame-thrower approaches the wrecked bridge across the Albert Canal at Canne, demolished by Belgian army engineers on May 10, 1940.

◄ Under fire from the 60 mm antitank gun in Casemate 17 at Eben Emael, Pioneers launch a large pneumatic boat for the hazardous journey across the Albert Canal. The Belgians were convinced that the canal would be an effective barrier against attacks by tanks and infantry.

Nazi Germany tried a re-run, they would enter Belgium to support them. Known as the Dyle Plan, it called for the French 1st, 2nd, and 7th Armies under Generals Blanchard, Huntziger, and Giraud respectively, and British Expeditionary Force (BEF) under Gort to advance into Belgium as far as the river Dyle. Here they would hold a line running from Antwerp through Louvain, Wavre, Namur, Dinant, to Monthermè on the Franco Belgian border. The Belgians aimed to defend their country by holding a line to the north based on the deep Albert Canal that ran from

▼ May 14, 1940, on the road to Waalhaven *Fallschirmjäger* (paratroops) of FJR 1 and air-landed troops of Infantry Regiment 16 prepare to move against the town center to capture key bridges.

▶ Infantry, some with vestigial helmet camouflage, await the order to advance protected by the dead ground of a roadside drainage ditch.

Antwerp to Maastricht and then along the Meuse to Namur and thence to Dinant. The key to these defenses was the modern fort of Eben Emael built at the southern end of the Albert Canal.

The chief of the general staff at the OKW, General Franz Halder, proposed a variant of the Schlieffen Plan. This would put the weight of the German attack through the "Maastricht Appendix," the strip of Dutch territory between southern Belgium and Germany. The battle would be fought in northern Belgium and trap the Anglo French armies against the Channel.

A variant of this idea put forward by General Erich von Manstein, the chief of staff to General von Rundstedt C-in-C Army Group A, would shift the weight further south so that the point where the full weight of the German assault, the *Schwerpunkt,* fell was at Sedan on the river Meuse. The three Panzer Corps, XV, XLI, and XIX, respectively under Generals Herman Hoth, Georg-Hans Reinhardt, and Heinz Guderian, would have to approach the French border through the wooded and mountainous roads of the Belgian Ardennes. French planners had asserted that if defended this was "tank proof" country.

▲ An NCO on the right watches as the crew of a 3.7 cm Pak 35/36 bring their gun forward. The weapon was one of the best anti-tank guns in the world until 1941, by which time 15,000 had been produced.

◀ Exhausted German infantry slump by the side of a French road. In 1940 German infantry were marching up to 100 kilometers a day as they followed up the fast moving panzer divisions. Some of the soldiers in this group have acquired bicycles to speed their advance.

▲ Infantry with an MG 34 crew supported by PzKpfw II and Czech-built PzKpfw 35(t) tanks move slowly through standing corn toward a distant skyline in May 1940.

▲ The first edition of *Signal* appeared in April 1940. The cover picture showed a camera crew in action in a burning town in Poland with a PzKpfw II in the background.

Because Belgium was neutral, the Franco Belgian border was not as heavily protected with concrete bunkers, barbed wire, and anti-tank obstacles. If the panzers and Stukas could punch through this thin skin, they could race through northern France to the Channel.

Von Rundstedt backed the new plan and its novelty appealed to Hitler. However in order to draw the Anglo French armies into Belgium the first moves would have to appear to be a re-run of the Schlieffen Plan. So as the panzers of Army Group A moved stealthily through Luxembourg and southern Belgium towards the Meuse, the men of Army Group B went into action against Holland and Belgium.

On paper the German forces were at near parity with the combined armies of France, Britain, Belgium, and the Netherlands. However pacifist governments had starved the Dutch army of weapons and equipment in the 1930s. It consisted of only eight divisions and reserves and incredibly, one tank. The Dutch airforce had 62 fighters and nine bombers. The Belgians had 18 divisions and reserves, a total of 900,000 men, and ten tanks. The airforce had 90 fighters and nine bombers. Opposite them across the border was Army Group B commanded by General Fedor von Bock. It consisted of 29 divisions of which three were panzer and two motorized.

▲ A PzKpfw II Ausf C armed with one 2 cm KwK 38 L/55 gun and one 7.92 mm machine gun. The tank with its crew of three had a maximum speed of 40 kmh on roads and cross-country range of 100 km.

◄ In a scene reminiscent of World War I, German ground crew steady an artillery observation balloon. A balloon out of range of AA fire would provide a stable platform for observing fall of shot.

The decisive balance in Germany's favor was her air force, 1,268 fighters, 1,120 level bombers, and 350 dive-bombers. The French *Armee de L'Air* could muster 700 fighters and 175 bombers. In France the Royal Air Force had 500 fighters and light bombers.

The German attack began on May 10, 1940, with air attacks on Dutch and Belgian airfields and airborne assaults on the bridges at Moerdijk and Rotterdam and the seat of government at The

▲ A flame thrower crew from Pioneer Battalion 51 commanded by *Feldwebel* Portsteffen attack a bunker at Eben Emael. The *Flammenwerfer* 35 had a range of 25 to 30 meters and duration of fire of ten seconds. The fuel container held 11.8 liters of oil.

Hague. With the bridges in German hands, the river line defenses of "Fortress Holland" were penetrated and, following a savage air attack on the city of Rotterdam, the Dutch capitulated on May 14.

Further south an èlite force from FJR 1, the German 1st Parachute Regiment, landed in ten gliders within the Belgian fort of Eben Emael and, using shaped charges, punched holes through the armored turrets of the gun emplacements. They neutralized

▶ One of the three triple casemates mounting 75 mm guns forming part of the sophisticated defenses of Eben Emael that covered the approaches to the fort.

◀ Soldiers from 151 German Infantry Regiment await relief as Belgian prisoners from Eben Emael huddle on the ground. *Signal* made much of this German victory.

the fort for 24 hours and were relieved by men of the 61st Infantry Division. Afterward, though photographs of the wrecked fort appeared in *Signal*, the Germans kept the techniques and tactics secret and the British were puzzled about how Eben Emael could have fallen so quickly. The Belgians had lost the Albert Canal Line and fell back on the Dyle Line as the French and British forces advanced to join them. The defense of the Low Countries was collapsing even before Germany had played her master-stroke.

▲ The shell pitted artillery, grenade projector, and machine-gun embrasures at Block 1, the entrance to Eben Emael. Within the gateway was a collapsible drawbridge designed to trap a tank if it attempted to break in through the entrance.

◀ Three symbolic graves with the helmets of a Belgian member of the garrison of Eben Emael and those of the victors—a paratrooper from *Storm Group Koch* and a soldier of either the 151 Infantry Regiment or Pioneer Battalion 51.

THE BATTLE OF FRANCE AND THE BATTLE OF BRITAIN

▲ A *Signal* cover for 1940 shows the cliffs near Dover with a Focke-Wulf Fw 58C *Weihe* liaison aircraft flying over patrolling E Boats in the English Channel.

"The next objective of our operations is to annihilate the French, English and Belgian forces which are surrounded in Artois and Flanders, by concentric attack by our northern flank and by the swift seizure of the Channel coast in this area. The task of the Luftwaffe will be to break all enemy resistance on the part of the surrounded forces, to prevent the escape of the English forces across the Channel."

—Adolf Hitler, *Directive No 13, May 24, 1940*

▲ Staggered casemates for 135 mm guns in the Maginot Line positioned to deliver flanking fire, sited so that they cannot be engaged with direct fire. The defenses were named after the French war minister, Andrè Maginot, who had served in World War I as a front-line sergeant. He believed that sophisticated defenses would be sufficient to protect France.

▲ Maginot Line garrison troops stand by for the arrival of a narrow gauge underground electric railway train. Tracks were laid in the main passageways to that the train could deliver ammunition or rations and move troops rapidly around the positions.

◀ PzKpfw I tanks scattered across the rolling cornfields of northern France. The tank was designed primarily as a training vehicle for drivers and gunners, but saw action in Spain during the Civil War and in Poland. It even saw action in 1941 in the invasion of Russia and soldiered on in a variety of roles until 1943.

OUT OF 8,410,000 MEN mobilized by France in World War I, some 1,385,300 had been killed and 4,266,000 wounded by 1918. The memories haunted the nation and war memorials in even the smallest villages listed the dead. As the prospect of a new conflict with Germany began to emerge the French looked to the lessons of World War I. The defense of Verdun had been costly for the French, but the Germans had suffered greater casualties attacking. France would build modern fixed defenses and remain secure behind them.

The line was named after the French minister of war, Andrè Maginot, who had been a sergeant in World War I. It was constructed between 1930 and 1935 and stretched from Switzerland to the Belgian border. The strongest areas were in the Metz region between Longuyon and Teting and the Lauter region between the Saar and Rhine rivers. It was garrisoned by 400,000 troops and consisted of artillery in depth with infantry bunkers closer to the German border. The existence of the Maginot Line made the French reluctant to consider offensive tactics and during the period of September 1939 to May 1940 only small-scale patrols into no-mans-land were undertaken. This time was nicknamed "Sitzkrieg" or the *Drole de Guerre (*the game of war). Morale and training suffered.

However, France had also developed armored and mechanized forces, and by 1940 the northeastern front had, with reserves and a Polish divisions, some 3,063 tanks. Though some were older designs dating back to World War I, there were others with thick armor and powerful guns. The tanks were concentrated in the northwest of France and as part of the Dyle plan moved into Belgium when the Germans attacked. Some elements of General Henri Giraud's 7th Army even attempted a dash across Belgium to assist the Dutch—it was going exactly as the Germans planned.

The Germans, having worked their way through Belgium and

▲ In the cold winter of 1939-40, a German patrol commander dressed in improvised winter camouflage. The binoculars made from aluminum alloy were light and had separately focusing eyepieces with a graticule for measuring ranges.

◄ With stick grenades at the ready a patrol moves through an evacuated village on the Franco-German border.

▼ Safely back in German territory the patrol moves towards its base.

Luxembourg protected by the *Luftwaffe,* reached the east bank of the Meuse on the evening of May 12. Guderian, commanding XIX Panzer Corps, knew that it was essential to keep the pressure on the French. Though his tanks were still reaching the river, supported by the Stukas of General Wolfram von Richthofen's VIII *Fliegerkorps,* he committed his assault troops and crossed the Meuse the following day seizing the adjoining high ground. By the evening, engineers had constructed bridges at Sedan. A door was open for the 1st, 2nd, and 10th Panzer Divisions. To the north at Monthermè, the XLI Panzer Corps under Reinhardt had established a bridgehead by May 15 and the 6th and 8th Panzer Divisions began their drive to the sea. At Dinant and

▲ An MG 34 crew takes up a position to cover the patrol. The Number Two on the gun holds the ammunition box with 250 rounds in a non-disintegrating belt.

Onhaye the XV Panzer Corps had achieved a lodgment across the Meuse by the 14th. The reconnaissance troops of General Erwin Rommel's 7th Panzer Division had found an unguarded weir and maneuvered their motorcycles carefully across the narrow walkway. The 5th Panzer Division joined the westward dash. To the north the XVI Panzer Corps under General Erich Höpner, actually part of Army Group B, swung left through Belgium and into northern France.

By May 16 the German salient was between 20 and 40 kilometers deep. There had been a brief delay at Montcornet on May 15 when an armored division commanded by General Charles de Gaulle attempted a counterattack. For the Germans the rivers Aisne and Somme covered their left flank as they pushed westward. On May 20 the tanks and motorcyclists of the 2nd Panzer Division reached the sea at Noyelles and the sickle cut trap had been sprung.

As the grasp on events of General Maurice Gamelin, the French commander in chief, was becoming weaker almost by the hour, the French and British under General Lord Gort attempted to coordinate a joint attack to cut through the German thrust. On May 21 tanks of the British 4th and 7th Royal Tank regiments with

▲ General Heinz Guderian in his SdKfz 251 half-track command vehicle. The picture was cropped by German censors to conceal the Enigma coding machine.

men of the 6th and 8th Durham Light Infantry struck Rommel's 7th Panzer Division and elements of the *Waffen-SS* Division *Totenkopf* near Arras. The shock was greater than the effect. Along with the tough resistance of Rifle Brigade and Queen Victoria Rifles at Calais, this may have been one of the factors that persuaded Hitler to issue an order not to press on to Dunkirk, an order that would change the course of the war forever.

The panzer divisions rolled up the channel coast capturing Boulogne on May 25 and trapping the British Expeditionary Force, Belgian Army, and French 1st Army in a pocket that included the Belgian port and resort town of Dunkirk. Initially the pocket, squeezed by tanks from Army Group A and infantry from Army Group B, reached from Gravelines on the coast in the west beyond Ostend in the east and as far as Valenciennes in the south. However with Belgium's surrender on the 28th, it shrunk rapidly to an area about 50 kilometers square. To the south the French 1st Army held a pocket near Lille until June 1 when it surrendered.

◀ One of only 280 PzKpfw IV Ausf A tanks (second from right) deployed in France and, PzKpfw 35(t)s and PzKpfw IIs wait the order to advance from the cover of dead ground close to the Somme River.

▶ Behind the tanks, headed by a Sd Kfz 223 armored car, the motorcycles and soft-skin vehicles with mechanized infantry wait to follow up the breakthrough.

▼ A PzKpfw III Ausf E tank advances through a bomb damaged village. Armed with a 3.7 cm gun, the 349 Mk IIIs that fought in France were decisive in the campaign.

▲ Having secured the village a young machine gunner draped with belted 7.92 mm rounds takes a breather.

It would have been easy work for the nine panzer divisions ranged along the western flank of the Dunkirk pocket to finish it off, but Hitler ordered a halt to the attacks and gave the responsibility for its destruction to the *Luftwaffe*. The tanks were redeployed south for the attack into France.

Through ULTRA intercepts, the British were aware that the Germans would not press their attack and this allowed Flag Officer Dover, Vice-Admiral Bertram Ramsay, to set in motion Operation *Dynamo*, the evacuation of the BEF from Dunkirk and the beaches. The operation began at 1900 on May 26 and ended at 0340 on June 4. Over 1,000 vessels including private pleasure craft, trawlers, and smaller warships lifted 338,000 British and French troops to safety in Britain. The cost was six British and three French destroyers sunk and 19 damaged, as well as 56 other ships and 161 small craft sunk. In dogfights over Dunkirk the RAF lost over 100 fighters, but downed a similar number of *Luftwaffe* aircraft.

◄ With a tactical gap between each man, German infantry sprints in to secure the burning village in northern France.

▶ Shocked French soldiers emerge with white flags from the village to surrender to the advancing German forces.

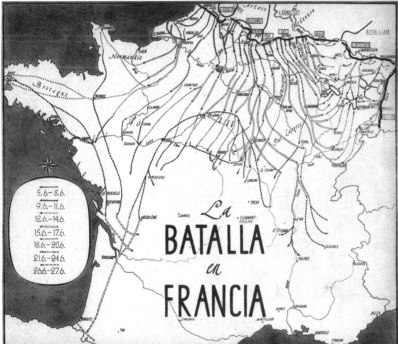

◄ A *Signal* map showing the Battle of France, the fast moving tank action that followed the fall of Dunkirk, which resulted in the capture of Paris and defeat of the remaining French forces.

On May 20 General Maxime Weygand replaced Gamelin and redeployed the French 2nd, 6th, 7th, and 10th Armies along the Somme. When the Germans launched the second phase of the attack on France on June 5, the French fought bravely but were severely weakened, and when the 14th and 16th Panzer Corps were held, the OKW simply re-deployed them and punched through further south. On the Channel coast the 5th and 7th

▲ A victory fanfare is sounded by a German corporal with a captured French trumpet while French prisoners are searched in the background.

▲ The cover of *Die Wehrmacht*, the official German army magazine, shows a PzKpfw 38(t) on the channel coast "*in position against England.*"

▶ A *Signal* photographer captures the confusion of the aftermath of a fire fight in a small French town. German soldiers hestitantly approach a mortally wounded French infantryman.

▲ A wrecked French destroyer, abandoned British 15 cwt Morris truck, and SMLE rifle and helmet on the beach at Dunkirk.

Panzer Divisions crossed the Seine at Rouen and reached Cherbourg and Brest on June 19.

The French government had now left Paris and the capital was declared an open city and entered by the Germans on June 14. Guderian's Panzer Group reached Pontarlier on the Swiss border on June 17 and by so doing trapped General Prètelat's French Army Group 2 against the Maginot Line. On June 22 the French were forced to surrender and accepted German terms in

◀ A menacing impression of the blitzkrieg in action. In the later years of the war the crew of an armored vehicle like this PzKpfw III would be at pains to avoid the narrow streets of a city or town, as this could be a death trap.

▶ Motorcycle dispatch riders pause by the smoking remains of a bombed building in downtown Dunkirk following the British withdrawal.

the railway carriage at Compiègne 50 miles northeast of Paris. This was the same carriage where the French Marshal Foch had accepted the surrender of German armies in November 1918— a symbolic revenge.

The new French government under Pierre Laval and Marshal Philippe Pètain based itself at the spa town of Vichy. Until November 1942, when German troops marched south to occupy this area officially known as the *Zone Libre*, or Free Zone, it was known as Vichy France. The Vichy government, much featured in *Signal*, was anti-British and existed even after the German occupation of its territory.

After the enormous losses of World War I the invasion of France seemed almost bloodless to the Germans. Total casualties for the army and *Luftwaffe* were 163,213 of whom 29,640 were dead. The French suffered 90,000 dead, 200,000 wounded, and 1.9 million taken prisoner of war.

Hitler had always had a nagging admiration for the British and assumed after the fall of France and evacuation of Dunkirk that Churchill's government would agree to surrender terms. When it did not, he set in motion the planning of *Fall Seelöwe* (Operation Sea Lion), an amphibious operation against Britain.

▲ Abandoned British Matilda Mk II tanks set alight by their crews to render them unusable by the German forces.

◀ PzKpfw 38(t) tanks herd a group of French prisoners. The Czech designed 38(t) had a crew of four and was armed with a Skoda A7 3.72 cm gun and two 7.92 CZ Type 37 machine guns. The tanks were taken over following the occupation of Czechoslovakia.

▶ A morose and bedraggled French prisoner talks to his German guard. The French were allowed to retain their gas masks and helmets in accordance with the Geneva Convention.

▲ As Foreign Minister Joachim von Ribbentrop looks on, Marshal Philippe Pètain, head of state of Vichy France, meets Hitler at Montoire in France on October 24, 1940.

The OKW had never considered in 1939 that they might invade Britain and so planning was undertaken in something of a rush. Shipping was assembled, and large barges were converted into landing craft. The *Kriegsmarine* proposed two major landing zones, one between Dover and Rye and the second between Brighton and Chichester, with a support landing near Weymouth. A revised plan had landings concentrated on beaches around Newhaven, Eastbourne, Hastings, Rye, Lydd, and Hythe. The initial phase would be to secure the South Downs, the second would see the 9th and 16th Armies reaching a line running from

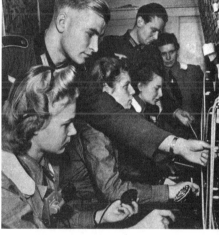

◀ In a symbolic posed picture a German MG 34 gunner stands guard at the foot of the Eiffel Tower in Paris. The staff of the tower sabotaged the elevator, so the Germans were obliged to climb stairs to reach the top in order to hoist the *Reichskriegsflagge* (Reich War Flag) over Paris.

▲ German army signalers brief female signals auxiliaries (*Nachrichtenhelferinnen*) on the intricacies of the military switchboard in Paris. The French nicknamed the women "gray mice" because of the color of their uniforms.

Portsmouth to Gravesend. The third phase would see the 16th Army isolating London and the 9th Army pushing north and west toward Oxford and Gloucester.

On the assumption of a successful operation against Britain, the *Sonderfahndungsliste–GB* (Special Search List–Great Britain), had been prepared by Walter Schellenberg of the *Reichssicherheitshauptamt*. Also known as the "Black Book," the list consisted of 2,300 prominent Britons and refugees who were to be arrested— among them scholars, writers, journalists, refugees from Germany and Europe, and even the playwright Noël Coward.

▲ Messerschmitt Bf 109E fighters, nicknamed by their crews "Emil," at standby on an airfield in northern France. This fighter design had earned a considerable reputation as a record single-seat aircraft when it was tested in prewar speed trials.

▲ A *Signal* photograph taken by a cameraman equipped with a telephoto lens shows Me 109s spread in the tactically flexible "fingers four" formation flying past a Chain Home radar station close to the chalk cliffs near Dover.

Before Operation *Seelöwe* could become a reality the *Luftwaffe* would have to achieve air superiority over the Channel and southern England to ensure that the Royal Navy could not disrupt the crossings. The air campaign through later summer and autumn of 1940, that to the British was known as the battle of Britain, cost the *Luftwaffe* 668 fighters and 700 bombers and other aircraft, and cost the Royal Air Force 832 fighters. Since most of the RAF pilots could land in England when their aircraft were shot down and return to service, while the *Luftwaffe* went into POW camps, the losses were actually more severe for the Germans.

The *Luftwaffe* deployed three Air Fleets *Luftflotte 2, Luftflotte 3,* and *Luftflotte 5* in France, Belgium, and Norway. A small Italian Air Force contingent also participated in the attacks on Britain and was featured in *Signal*.

The battle fell into five phases: July 10–August 7 the preliminary phase; August 8–23 attacks on coastal targets; August 24–September 6 attacks on Fighter Command airfields; September 7–30 daylight attacks on London chiefly by medium bombers; and October 1–31 attacks on London chiefly by fighter bombers.

◄ Me 109 fighters on patrol on the coast. Air-to-air photographs of single-seat fighters such as the Me 109 are less common in *Signal* than those of bombers or the two-seater Me 110 where gunners or other crew members were in a position to take pictures.

▲ A *Signal* cover that purports to show a *Luftwaffe* bomber pilot at the moment he realizes that an RAF Spitfire is closing in for the attack.

◄ An RAF Spitfire in a dispersal bay is caught in a burst of cannon fire by a low flying fighter. The *Luftwaffe* attacks on the RAF airfields were beginning to reduce its strength and capability, but then they switched to the cities.

◄ A photo sequence from *Signal* shows bombs falling from a Dornier Do 17Z as it unloads its 1,000-kg payload during a daylight raid over Britain.

▲ The crew of a Junkers Ju 88A-1 of the 3rd Staffel Kg 51 "*Edelweiss*" based at Melun-Villaroche prepares for a mission in August 1940.

For the RAF the build up of pressure allowed pilots, ground crew, and fighter controllers to become experienced at handling interceptions. For the *Luftwaffe* the main assault took place on *Adlertag* (Eagle Day) when they flew 1,485 sorties losing 45 aircraft to the RAF's 13.

The two principal *Luftwaffe* fighters were the Messerschmitt Bf 109 and the Messerschmitt Bf 110. Designed in 1935 the "one-o-nine" first saw action in Spain in 1939 and remained in production until 1945. Armament for the Bf 109E was three 20 mm cannon and two 7.92mm machine guns.

An unsuccessful two seater, the Me 110 twin-engined fighter was surprisingly featured widely in *Signal,* though this may have been a move to "sell" it to the readers. Its armament was typically two 30 mm cannon, two 20 mm cannon, and two 7.92 mm machine guns, and it could carry 1,000 kg of bombs.

The *Luftwaffe* bombers were the Junkers Ju 88 that had a 3,000 kg bomb capacity, the Heinkel He III with 2,500 kg capacity, and the Dornier Do-17 with a 910 kg bomb capacity. The slow-flying Junkers Ju 87 Stuka, with its 500 kg bomb load,

▲ A Ju 88, an aircraft type that served as a bomber in the battle of Britain and later as a night fighter in 1943–45 and as a flying bomb at the close of the war.

◄ A damaged Messerschmitt Bf 110C or D ditched in the Channel close to France. The photograph, which is part of a sequence in *Signal,* covers an air–sea rescue operation. The Me 110 was designated a *Zerstörer* or Destroyer, but its formidable armament of four 7.92 machine guns and two 20-mm cannon was no compensation for its slow speed and poor maneuverability.

▶ The distinctive glazed nose of a Heinkel He IIIP bomber which carried a crew of four, had a range of 2,000 km, and had an external and internal bomb load of 2,000 kg.

▲ The tail fin of a Focke-Wulf Fw 200C Condor maritime patrol bomber showing "kills" against British shipping in the North Atlantic. Condors sank 85 merchant ships in five months during 1940–41.

had proved effective as a dive-bomber in France and Poland but was vulnerable to antiaircraft fire and particularly fighter attack.

The RAF deployed the Hawker Hurricane and Supermarine Spitfire, both armed with eight .303 Browning machine guns. There were 19 Spitfire squadrons and their role was to keep the escorting *Luftwaffe* fighters away from the Hurricanes as they went for the bombers. Hurricanes made up 60 percent of RAF Fighter Command in the battle and consequently shot down the largest number of enemy aircraft.

War photographers flying in *Luftwaffe* bombers provided *Signal* with dramatic air-to-air photographs of air combat. Though the RAF was a threat, the pictures and maps showed that the bombers were getting through to their targets. But the value of the Chain Home radar system and ULTRA intelligence

◀ Running the gauntlet of air attacks, British coasters, taken in another *Signal* telephoto image, sail up the Channel. The opening phases of the battle of Britain lasted from June to August. Though 30,000 tons of shipping were sunk, some one million passed safely through the Channel to deliver valuable cargo to the London Docks.

was critical for allowing the RAF to anticipate attacks and intercept bomber squadrons often before they had reached their targets.

In the winter of 1940–41 the *Luftwaffe* changed tactics and began to bomb urban targets in the assumption that the RAF was broken, and to avenge attacks on Berlin by RAF bombers. The first raid on London was on September 7–8, 1940. The most severe was against Coventry on November 14–15 in which 550 people were killed, over 1,200 wounded, and 60,000 buildings destroyed. *Signal* featured the attack and the macabre term coined by Dr. Goebbels—in the future cities would be "Coventrized."

By the spring of 1941, Hitler was planning the attack on Russia and *Luftwaffe* bomber and fighter squadrons were moved from France to Poland. The invasion threat for Britain was over but the blitz had cost 40,000 civilian deaths with 46,000 injured.

▲ He IIIP bombers in close formation. The aircraft was powered by two 1,020 hp Daimler-Benz DB 601Aa engines that being unsynchronized had a distinctive throbbing "beat" grimly familiar to the British civilians.

▼ In a *Signal* picture story a Junkers Ju 88 crew prepares for a night mission. The day and night "blitz" bomber attacks against the cities of Britain killed civilians and wrecked homes, but took the pressure off the RAF installations and airfields.

GREECE, THE BALKANS AND NORTH AFRICA

> "As a base for air warfare against Great Britain in the Eastern Mediterranean we must prepare to occupy the island of Crete (Unternehmen Merkur)."
>
> —Adolf Hitler, *Directive No 28, April 25, 1941*

◀ Max Schmeling, Germany's most successful heavyweight boxer and champion of the world from 1930 to 1932, became a paratrooper and was given star status in *Signal.*

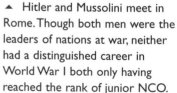

▲ Hitler and Mussolini meet in Rome. Though both men were the leaders of nations at war, neither had a distinguished career in World War I both only having reached the rank of junior NCO.

HITLER HAD BEEN an early admirer of the fascist Italy of Benito Mussolini. Long before he had achieved power in Germany in 1933, Mussolini had begun to transform Italy into a totalitarian state. Italy went to war to seize the African kingdom of Abyssinia in October 1935 and had expanded its territorial and colonial control through the 1930s.

Italy declared war on France on June 10, 1940, as the French were reeling from the attacks by German panzer divisions. The Italian attempt to advance along the Mediterranean coast was disastrous and the depleted French forces held the attacks until the French surrender at Compiégne. The Italians were then able to grab border areas of southeastern France and extended their control as far as Lyon to the north and Avignon to the south on the River Rhone, as well as on the island of Corsica.

On September 27, 1940, Germany and Italy, who had already signed the Axis Pact on May 22, 1939, signed the Tripartite Pact

▲ Hunched in their waterproof coats the crew of a BMW 746 cc R75 motorcycle combination drive along a Yugoslavian road flooded by spring rains. The combination had a maximum road speed of 92 kmh.

▲ German engineers take cover behind concrete antitank obstacles placed along the Greek-Bulgarian border. Since the obstacles were not protected by barbed wire, the engineers could easily demolish or remove them.

▶ A *Signal* photograph of Italian troops street fighting in southern France. Many Italian troops later fought bravely in the Balkans, but poor leadership and obsolescent equipment, as well as severe weather, made it a harsh campaign.

▶ A *Signal* back cover photograph shows the commander and gunner/radio operator of a PzKpfw II perched on the turret as the driver negotiates a swollen stream in Yugoslavia. The crew wear lightweight overalls and the black panzer *feldmütze* side cap that entered service in 1940.

▲ A PzKpfw III drives along a mountain pass in the Balkans. Later in the war defiles like this would be ideal ambush sites and potential death traps as partisans fought a war in which neither side offered pity or quarter.

with Japan that promised mutual assistance if one of the signatories was attacked. In November, Romania, Hungary, and Slovakia signed the pact, and in March 1941 Bulgaria and Yugoslavia followed. Yugoslavia repudiated the pact almost immediately following a coup. The Nazi puppet state of Croatia signed on June 15, 1941. *Signal* would make much of these European allies as well as men and women from occupied Europe who volunteered to serve with the German armed forces.

◀ *Gebirgsjäger* (mountain troops) lead mules laden with radio equipment along a mountain track. German mountain troops had a range of specialized lightweight weapons and equipment that could be broken down into loads transportable by mule or even man.

▼ Well-spaced, a patrol makes its way across high ground in Yugoslavia. Simple fieldcraft skills like spacing made them harder targets for area weapons like mortars and artillery and difficult to locate at a distance.

▲ A 3.7 cm Pak 35/36 antitank gun crew cover the border crossing from Bulgaria into Greece. In action the gun weighed 328 kg and could fire both HE and AP ammunition.

The Tripartite Pact did not include joint measures for waging the war and left member states some leeway. So though Italian troops had invaded the tiny and primitive kingdom of Albania as far back as April 7, 1939, Mussolini caught Hitler off guard when he announced, "Führer we are on the march," and informed him that Italian troops in Albania had attacked Greece on October 28, 1940. The Italians made some headway but in bitter weather the Greeks counterattacked on November 4 and eventually forced them out of Greece and across the border into Albania.

At sea the Italian navy was suffering humiliating losses in action against the Royal Navy in the Mediterranean. In Operation *Judgement*, Fleet Air Arm Swordfish carrier torpedo bombers had

crippled battleships in their base at Taranto on November 11, 1940. On March 28, 1941, at the battle of Cape Matapan, ULTRA intelligence allowed the British Mediterranean fleet to damage the battleship *Vittorio Veneto*, and sink two heavy cruisers and two destroyers, while the damaged heavy cruiser *Pola* was later torpedoed.

After pushing into Egypt with 80,000 men on September 13, 1940, the Italian army was counterattacked on December 10–11 by a fast moving and vigorously led British and Common-wealth force of 30,000 commanded by General Archibald Wavell, and were forced back into Libya. On February 7 at Beda Fomm, a pincer movement caught the withdrawing Italians and by the end of their campaign they had lost 130,000 troops, 845 guns, and 380 tanks while British and Commonwealth losses numbered 2,000 men.

Through Germany's Italian ally was described in glowing arti-cles and captions in *Signal*, in reality it was becoming a liability.

Hitler was well advanced in his plans for the invasion of Russia and when, in March 1941, British troops and aircraft arrived in Greece he knew that his right flank would have to be secured. Romania was now supplying Germany with the bulk of its fuel and oil requirements from the Ploesti oil fields, and bombers based in a hostile Greece could easily reach this key target in Romania.

▲ (Left) Paratroopers march out to their Ju 52 transports. Their major role would be in the attack on Crete, but 52 parachute engineers and two battalions from FJR 2 would be committed to the capture of bridges across the Corinth Canal on April 25, 1941.(Center) *Gebirgsjäger* with their distinctive *Bergmütze* caps wait on an airfield in Greece. The cap was based on the design of the Austrian army service cap and in cold conditions the flaps could be unbuttoned and folded down to cover the wearer's ears.

The fastest and most effective way to prevent this was to neutralize Greece. A passive or cooperative Yugoslavia was necessary for German troops to move south. The Yugoslav government in Belgrade was strong-armed by the Germans and Italians into joining the Tripartite Pact on March 25. But encouraged by the British Foreign Office, Prince Paul of Yugoslavia led a coup against the government, rejecting the pact. This triggered an air attack on Belgrade named Operation Punishment by Hitler, that killed 5,000 people in a supposedly open city and panicked the young king and his government into flight. The campaign opened on April 6 with the German 2nd Army under General Freiherr von Weichs attacking from Austria and General von Kleist's 1st *Panzergruppe,* that had been earmarked for an attack on Thrace in Greece, pushing towards Belgrade from Bulgaria. The 12th Army attacked Thrace, detaching the 40th *Panzer Korps* westward through the Vardar region of southern Yugoslavia that led to Macedonia and the Monastir gap.

On April 12 German forces met up with the Italians and moved toward Greece. A day later in a daring coup, Belgrade was occupied by motorcycle reconnaissance troops of the *Waffen-SS* Division *Das Reich*. Three days later an armistice was signed that created a puppet state of Croatia and placed the rest of Yugoslavia under Italian or Hungarian rule or German martial law.

▲ German troops with captured Greek vehicles muster on the harbor front at Kavalla on the northern Aegean. Following the Greek surrender in Athens, Italy and Germany jointly garrisoned Greece and its offshore islands.

▲ German soldiers maneuver a motorcycle combination over rough ground. The motorcycle and side car with its two-or three-man team and an MG 34 could be a small but formidable force.

▶ With Mount Olympus in the background, an MG 34 crew serves duty as antiaircraft sentries with an observer and one man holding the AA mount to keep it stable.

With Bulgaria within the Nazi orbit the Greek defenses in front of Albania known as the Metaxas Line could be outflanked through Thrace. The German attack on Greece in April 8 was codenamed *Unternehmen Marita* (Undertaking Marita). The original operation in a directive from Hitler in December 13, 1940, called for the occupation of the Aegean coast and Salonika Basin and the offshore islands. The operation was quick and ruthless and the 12th Army under Wilhem von List pierced the Greek defenses in Thrace and took Salonika. The 40th Panzer Korps, pushing through the Monastir Gap from Yugoslavia, hit the British forces covering the approaches from Bulgaria. In a fighting withdrawal they held the Germans at Thermopylae on April 24. This action and the access to ULTRA decrypts allowed the British to second guess the German moves and evacuate, not only many of their men, but also King George of Greece. German forces reached Athens on April 27 and the German love affair with ancient Greece was given a new character as propaganda company photographers recorded the moment the *Reichskriegsflagge* was run up on a flagstaff on the Acropolis.

The campaign in Greece and Yugoslavia was a triumph for the German tactics of coordinating tanks, mechanized infantry, and dive-bombers. Germans lost 558 casualties in Yugoslavia and 4,500 in Greece; the British, who had committed 75,000 to the campaign, lost 10,000 men as prisoners; the Yugoslavs lost 90,000 men, and the Greeks, who were fully mobilized, lost 270,000 men. Photographs in *Signal* showed the Yugoslav army

A *Signal* picture spread of Dornier Do 17Z bombers in formation over the Acropolis in central Athens following it's capture on April 27, 1941.

An SdKfz 231 armored car armed with a 2-cm KwK cannon and 7.92-mm machine gun passes the Greek parliament building in Athens after the Greek surrender.

German soldiers raise the *Reichskriegsflagge* over the Acropolis. The colors of black, white, and red in the flag date back to the imperial heyday of the 1860s.

▶ Paratroopers suspended from their RZ20 parachutes float away from a Ju52. The paratroopers hung from the harnesses in a face down position and landed making a forward roll. They wore padded guards to protect their knees and padded gauntlets. The rubber soled high boots also afforded support and protection.

▲ *Fallschirmjäger* (paratroops) dash to collect weapons from a *Waffenbehälter* (weapons container). These containers were packed with weapons and equipment and marked with colored rings and bars to indicate their content. A section of twelve paratroopers required four arms containers which were released at the moment the men jumped.

as a pitiful organization traumatized by the violence of the blitzkrieg.

The final stage in the German occupation of Greece was the attack on Crete on May 20–23, 1941, a unique battle named *Unternehmen Merkur* (Undertaking Mercury). The Germans committed 17,530 men by glider, transport plane, and parachute to the capture of the island. It was defended by 35,000 British and Commonwealth forces, however many men on the island had been evacuated from the Greek mainland and had limited weapons, ammunition, transport, and poor communications equipment.

The Germans had complete air superiority. However the

▲ Parachutes fill the air over Crete at the launch of Operation *Merkur*. The *Luftwaffe* had introduced a camouflaged canopy in time for the airborne assault.

◀ Mountain infantry, who had been flown into Maleme airfield after it had been secured by paratroops, move eastward across the island.

British and Commonwealth troops commanded by a New Zealander, General Bernard Freyberg, had a unique advantage of being familiar with German plans through ULTRA intercepts. They knew where the proposed four drop zones were located in Crete at Maleme, Herakleion, Canea, and Retimo, and were able

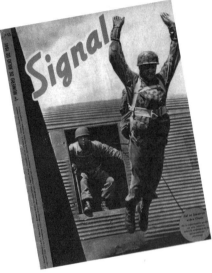

▶ The distinctive shape of *Tante Ju* (Auntie Junkers). The Ju 52 delivered troops and supplies and as a *Sani Ju* operated as an air ambulance which carried 12 litters.

◀ Two of the three reliable 830-hp BMW 132T-2 radial engines that gave the Ju 52 a top speed of 286 kph at 1,400 meters and a range of 1,500 kilometers.

◀ A spectacular cover of *Signal* shows the diving exit necessary to avoid snagging the static line on the tailplane of the Ju 52.

▼ A *Luftwaffe* motorcycle combination crew gaze at a Ju 52. Its port wing is ripped from its mountings and it has crash-landed close to the Maleme airfield in Crete.

to engage the *Fallschirmjäger* as they were still in the air. Because Freyberg did not want to compromise his ULTRA intelligence by exactly second guessing the German moves as a cover he also positioned troops on the coast.

Through lack of resources the British and Commonwealth forces were unable to win the battle, but they killed 7,000 German paratroops, 2,000 Germans were reported missing, and some 370 aircraft were destroyed or damaged. The British and Commonwealth losses were 1,742 killed and missing, and 2,225 wounded, with 11,370 captured.

The evacuation of the garrison by the Royal Navy cost three cruisers and six destroyers sunk, but when it ended on June 1, 16,500 men had been saved. *Signal* featured dramatic pictures of Stuka attacks on the Royal Navy off Crete. However so severe were the losses at Crete that the Germans never attempted a major airborne operation again. The *Fallschirmjäger* would fight on through the war as elite infantry.

The aircraft that the *Fallschirmjäger* flew towards Crete were the Junkers Ju 52. A tough and reliable aircraft, the Ju 52 enjoyed nicknames like "Iron Annie" (*Judula*) or "Auntie Junkers" (*Tante Ju*). The slab-sided, three-motored aircrafts with a striking corrugated metal fuselage and wings had crews of two or three. They each carried 12 parachutists or 17 men, though in emergencies they were often overloaded.

▶ A 4 x 4 AU/Horch or Opel *Einheitsfahrgestell für mittlerer Personenkraftwagen* (Efm m.E.Pkw), heads an *Afrika Korps* parade in Tripoli in February 1941. The m.E.Pkw medium car was a heavy and demanding vehicle requiring excessive maintenance with almost 100 grease nipples that needed regular attention.

▲ An 8 x 8 SdKfz 231 *schwere Panzer Spähwagen* armored car on parade in Tripoli. With a crew of four this heavy armored car was also produced as a signals vehicle, SdKfz 232 and SP gun SdKfz 233.

While the Balkans campaign was being fought, on the other side of the Mediterranean Germany was again coming to the assistance of its unreliable ally. The Italians had been driven back deep into their colony of Libya by British and Commonwealth forces and so Berlin decided that a small force should be sent to assist them. It was called the *Deutsches Afrika Korps* (DAK) or *Afrika Korps* and consisted of the 15th Panzer and 5th Light (later renamed 21st Panzer) Divisions, though the title would be used for all German forces serving in North Africa from 1941 to 1943.

▶ With Italian officers, Rommel takes the salute of the newly arrived *Deutsches Afrika Korps* on February 27, 1941. The parade was prominently featured in *Signal* as an example of joint Axis operations in Africa.

▲ A PzKpfw III is swung ashore in Tripoli from a camouflaged freighter. German tanks would prove superior to British designs.

▲ A 4 x 4 Kfz AU/Horch 40 five-seat medium car, Rommel's favored staff car, heads a convoy as it leaves the dock front at Tripoli.

▼ A *Luftwaffe* motorcyclist changes the tire on an Italian Moto Guzzi Alce sidecar unit. All the wheels on the Alce were interchangeable.

▶ Rommel eats a snack in a Kfz 70 Horch. A Kar 98 K rifle is in the weapons rack. His captured British anti-gas goggles looped around his cap became the trade mark of the "Desert Fox."

▲ In a brand new tropical uniform and the short-lived *Tropische Kopfbedeckung* (sun helmet), the commander of the *Afrika Korps* dismounts from a captured British Mk VI Crusader I cruiser tank. Rommel's picture in color and black and white was featured on many *Signal* covers and in feature articles.

The *Afrika Korps* was commanded by Lt. General Erwin Rommel, a soldier who would be as much respected by his British and Commonwealth enemies, who nicknamed him the "Desert Fox," as by the soldiers under his command. Rommel, who had served with distinction in World War I, commanded the *Afrika Korps* from February 6, 1941, to March 9, 1943, during which time he outfought the British and Commonwealth forces on numerous occasions.

For *Signal* the *Afrika Korps* and operations in North Africa had a huge appeal. Rommel, the dashing commander of the DAK, was widely featured. Joint operations by Italian and German troops also made good propaganda pictures.

Rommel was an aggressive and energetic leader and before his forces were fully up to strength he elected to attack. The Germans hit the British positions at Al Agheila on March 24, and as the exhausted British forces fell back the DAK roamed deep into the desert. Benghazi fell on April 4, Derna on the 7th, and Rommel reached

Conventional and exotic transport for the *Afrika Korps*—camels were rarely used but this romantic image was probably irresistable to the readers as well as the editorial staff of *Signal*. The other two images are more realistic, showing the foot patrol or vehicle convoys, well spaced against air attacks.

▶ An *Afrika Korps* crew fires a 7.5-cm *leichtes Infanteriegeschütz* 18. This light infantry gun fired a 6 kg or 5.45 kg shell out to 3,550 meters.

◀ This picture of a soldier of the *Afrika Korps* on the cover of the Dutch language edition of *Signal* in 1941 summed up two of the problems of North Africa—sun and sand storms.

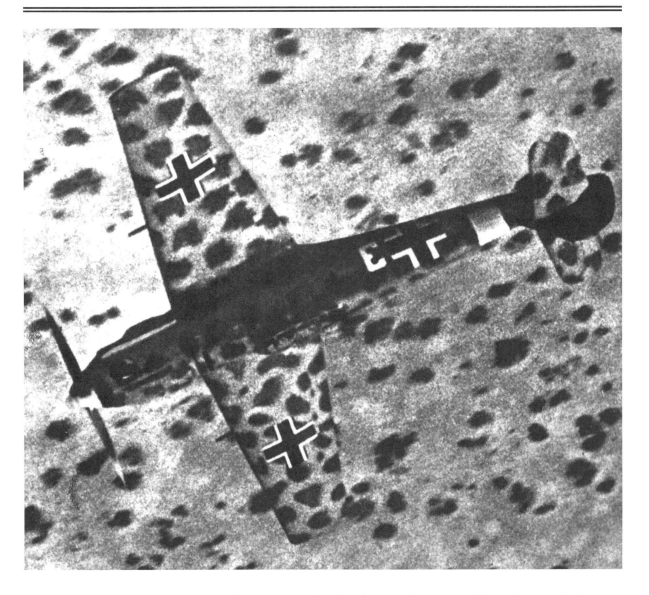

▲ This striking back cover picture from *Signal* of a Bf 109F-2/Trop of I *Gruppe Jagdgeschwader* 27 was printed upside down, suggesting it was looping the loop. The photograph shows how effective the camouflage of green on a tan background was against the sand and desert scrub.

the Egyptian border by April 25. But the Italian and German forces lacked the strength to take the port of Tobruk that was cut off on April 10, and it held for six months, supplied at night by sea deep behind Axis lines.

The *Afrika Korps* survived two operations mounted by General Wavel Brevity on May 15 and Operation Battleaxe on June 15. Both were attempts to relieve Tobruk. His successor General Claude Auchinleck, commanding an enlarged British and Commonwealth force renamed the 8th Army, launched Operation Crusader on November 18, 1941. The 8th Army now had over 700 tanks while the *Afrika Korps* was reduced to 320 of which nearly half were Italian. The attack initially achieved

◀ A fuel drum is rolled out to a Bf 109 on a desert airfield. Lack of fuel for aircraft and vehicles would dog *Afrika Korps* operations throughout the campaign. Submarine and air attacks against Axis convoys that cut the supply of fuel were based on ULTRA intelligence.

▼ Dressed in shorts and sun helmets, a *Luftwaffe* ground crew prepares to winch an SC1000 heavy calibre bomb onto the external rack of an He 111.

◀ Ground crew lounge in deck chairs as they shelter from the sun under the wing of a Bf 109 fighter of *Jagdgeschwader* 53 "Pik As." The canopy is open on the fighter and a sunshade has been positioned to keep the cockpit cool.

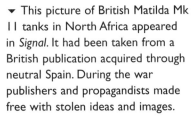

▼ This picture of British Matilda Mk II tanks in North Africa appeared in *Signal*. It had been taken from a British publication acquired through neutral Spain. During the war publishers and propagandists made free with stolen ideas and images.

The *Afrika Korps* tank killers. (Top) A 5-cm Pak 38 in position behind a sand bag sangar. The Pak 38 firing a tungsten core 0.925 kg AP40 could penetrate nearly all types of Allied heavy tanks. Firing HE, it had a range of 2,650 meters. (Above) The 8.8-cm *Flugabwehrkanone* 18 in action. The "Eighty Eight" was originally an antiaircraft gun, but with a muzzle velocity of 820 to 840 meters a second firing 9.6 kg solid shot, it was lethal against all tanks.

complete surprise but Rommel's quick reactions nearly destroyed the British plan. However on December 4 the 8th Army had punched through to relieve Tobruk.

At the start of February 1942, the 8th Army dug itself into positions in Gazala. But outmaneuvered by the *Afrika Korps* and heavily defeated in June 1942, the 8th Army retreated from Cyrenaica. This time Rommel was able to take Tobruk on June 21 and push on towards Egypt. *Signal* photographs of the depressed faces of captured Indian and African troops of the 8th Army contrasted with the fresh-faced men of the *Afrika Korps*.

Rommel's forces arrived at the Alamein area on June 30 and caused panic in Cairo. Auchinleck however fought him to a stand-still and by July 3 the *Afrika Korps* had only 26 tanks fit for action. Churchill, aware that commanders in North Africa had

▶ A blast from the versatile Infantry 7.5 cm LeIG 18 guns kicks up dust as they open fire and (below right) a German soldier shelters from the harsh sun behind a simple stone defense known as a "sangar."

▲ Italian troops of the *Bersaglieri* escort two British prisoners to the rear. The British soldiers retained their greatcoats because night time can be cold in the desert.

◀ An *Afrika Korps* soldier examines a knocked out British Crusader tank. The Crusader had a crew of five and was armed with an ineffective 2-pdr gun.

▲ An Italian Savoia-Marchetti S.M.79-II *Sparviero* (Sparrow Hawk) bomber flies across the Mediterranean. The aircraft, with a crew of four or five, was powered by three 780 hp Alfa Romeo 126 RC 34 engines had a maximum range of 1,900 km, and a bomb load of 1,250 kg.

▶ This photo of a Pz Kpfw Mk III shows the devastation caused by internal explosions from mine damage and antitank gunfire.

▲ *Signal* photographers captured a relaxed Italian ground crew as they load 12.7-mm ammunition into a Macchi MC.200 *Saetta* (Lightning fighter.) It was armed with two SAFAT machine guns and powered by a 870 hp Fiat A.74 RC 38 engine with a top speed of 502 kmh at 4,500 meters.

access to ULTRA intelligence, was impatient at the apparent lack of progress and on August 13 replaced Auchinleck with General Harold Alexander as commander in chief in the Middle East. General Bernard Montgomery took command of the 8th Army.

Rommel's final throw was the battle of Alam Halfa on August 30. He now had 200 German and 240 vulnerable Italian tanks. The 8th Army had 700 tanks, many of which were modern American Grants or Shermans. With the benefit of ULTRA,

In the dawn chill (above left) an Italian soldier searches a captured South African. In a posed picture (above) a British soldier surrenders from a knocked out Matilda Mk II tank. Images like this in *Signal* reinforced an illusion of triumph in Africa.

Montgomery anticipated an attempt to outflank the 8th Army and the Axis forces were halted by September 2. Stymied, the *Afrika Korps* dug in to await the 8th Army.

By October 23, 1942, Rommel had 80,000 men and 540 tanks of which 280 were Italian and only 38 the superior PzKpfw IV. Montgomery having resisted pressure from Churchill for an earlier attack had amassed 230,000 men and 1,200 tanks including 500 Grants or Shermans. It was time for the final show down between the 8th Army and the *Afrika Korps*.

▲ A captured soldier wearing the characteristic South African army sun helmet on the cover of the magazine *Die Wehrmacht*.

BARBAROSSA

"The war with Russia will be such that it cannot be conducted in a chivalrous fashion. This struggle is one of ideologies and racial differences and will be conducted with unprecedented merciless and unrelenting harshness."

—Adolf Hitler to senior officers, *March 1941*

▲ A *Signal* cover encapsulates the destruction of war showing troops advancing through a burning village.

▶ In the mists of June 22 men of the German 4th Army cross the bridge over the Bug River in the opening hours of Operation Barbarossa. The broad rivers of Eastern Europe were to play a critical part in operations by both sides in that theater.

◀ Almost invisible even in open ground soldiers move forward through the agricultural land of eastern Poland. This territory was grabbed by the Soviet Union in 1939 as a buffer against attacks from the west, but fast moving armored columns soon reached the Soviet border.

THE INVASION OF RUSSIA at dawn on June 22, 1941, literally caught the Russians napping. Border guards were captured semi-clothed as they stumbled half awake out of their barracks. It was the war that had long been predicted, even though Nazi Germany and the Soviet Union had signed a non-aggression pact in 1939. For Hitler the drive on the east was the expansion that would give the Germans *lebensraum* (living space), a concept he had first proposed in the book *Mein Kampf* (*My Struggle*) that became a Nazi "Bible."

The plans had been drafted as far back as December 6, 1940, with the code name *Fall Fritz* (Plan Fritz), however on December 18 Hitler changed the name. It would be *Unternehmen Barbarossa* (Operation Barbarossa), or Red Beard, the hero of the Holy Roman Empire who led the Third Crusade and died in Asia Minor.

▼ Relaxed German soldiers are ferried across a river in pneumatic assault boats—these are clearly follow up forces that are moving forward to consolidate the territory captured in the first assaults.

Signal photographers show the violence of the battle for the bunkers of the Soviet border defenses. Massive charges or close range artillery fire have smashed through the reinforced concrete and infantry storm into the breach.

▶ Well camouflaged among the woodland, bunkers had to be located and then neutralized by Pioneers with pole charges that were pushed through the embrasures.

▼ *Signal* captures the look of intense concentration of the helmsman's face as he steers a *Sturmboot* across a river toward the enemy bank. The boat, capable of lifting seven men and their equipment, carries an MG 34 crew.

In June 1941 German troops, with their Romanian, Finnish, Hungarian, and Slovak allies, began to make these ideas a reality as they punched eastward deep into the Soviet Union. The attack was split between three Army Groups. Army Group North under Field Marshal Ritter von Leeb consisted of seven divisions and three panzer divisions; Army Group Center under Field Marshal Fedor von Bock had 42 divisions and nine panzer divisions; and Army Group South under Field Marshal Gerd von Rundstedt had 52 divisions of which

▼ In a *Signal* spread a 3.7 cm Pak crew takes on a defended building at close range. The pressed steel ammunition boxes for the HE and AP ammunition can be seen on the ground behind the crew.

A *Luftwaffe* ground crew directs a Stuka as it taxies following a sortie.

▲ Bombed, burned, and blasted, a convoy of Soviet ZIS-32 4x4 3-ton trucks smolders after a Stuka attack near Kiev. The ZIS-32 had a maximum speed of 60 to 65 kmh on surfaced roads.

▲ Ju 87 dive-bombers begin to peel off to attack a target. Though they could deliver a 500 kg bomb with great accuracy, the howl of the wind through their dive brakes and even special sirens was terrifying to troops on the ground—it was nicknamed the "Trumpet of Jericoh."

fifteen were Romanian, two Hungarian, two Italian plus five panzer divisions. The Army Groups were supported by nine lines of communications divisions and over 3,000 aircraft.

The Soviet forces opposite them were grouped in three fronts the North-Western, Western, and the South-West, and consisted of 158 divisions with 54 tank brigades; however they had huge reserves and within six months 300 new divisions had been equipped from new factories in the Urals and mobilized.

In the air and on the ground the *Luftwaffe* destroyed 3,000 aircraft, nearly half the Red Air Force, in the first few days of June 1941. The tactical bombers attacked road and rail communications, destroyed headquarters, and could even bomb small targets like bunkers and trench lines. The Ju 87 Stuka close-support dive-bomber became the flying artillery of the men on the ground.

Though the opening months of the war in the East were a disaster for the USSR and its leader Joseph Stalin, geography favored the Soviet Union. Whereas in the West the German panzer divisions were able to advance on surfaced roads and the distances between objectives like ports, airfields, and cities was in tens or hundreds of miles, in the USSR roads were dirt tracks that linked cities that were vast distances apart. Dust, mud, and later extreme cold would take a toll of men and machines. The German army would also not be well served by Hitler, who would eventually take on the rank of commander in chief of the Armed Forces, increasingly interfere, reduce tactical flexibility, and as a result cause needless casualties. Even before the operation was launched there was a conflict of views over priorities.

▲ With its rear decks cluttered with spare kits and an extra length of tank track, a PzKpfw III grinds through the dust of a Belorussian road. In the heat the crew have opened the turret side hatches to allow more air to circulate.

▲ Crudely camouflaged Polikarpov I-15 fighters seized almost undamaged at a Red Air Force. Twenty-two captured aircraft were supplied to Finland, Germany's ally.

▸ A PzKpfw III, with the "K" of Panzer Gruppe Kleist and its turret with markings that identify it as the Regimental Adjutant's tank, engages a Soviet soft-skin vehicle with machine-gun fire.

▲ General Guderian, known as "Fast Heinz" to his troops, issues quick orders in a roadside conference. In 1941 the German army was a flexible and hugely experienced force well able to seize tactical opportunities as soon as they appeared.

The first plan drafted by General Marcks, the chief of staff of the 18th Army, envisaged a twin thrust at Moscow and Kiev. A huge encircling battle could be fought as the Moscow thrust swung south and linked up with the Kiev axis at Kharkov. General Halder, chief of the OKW, proposed an attack that spread the weight more equally between the north, center, and south but made Moscow the main objective. Hitler proposed that Leningrad, "the cradle of the Bolshevik revolution," should be the main objective and Moscow should be taken subsequently.

Optimistic German planners envisaged holding a line from Archangel in the north to Astrakhan in the south, the A–A line, by the onset of winter in 1941. Optimism and ignorance also featured in the assessment of the severity of the Russian winter. Men were woefully ill-equipped and the lubricants and grease in their weapons on equipment froze. In the winter of 1941–42 the German army suffered 133,620 frostbite casualties.

German tank and mechanized infantry in fast-moving panzer divisions outmaneuvered the Soviet armies, cut them off, and surrounded them in huge pockets, *kessels* or cauldrons. On July 3 near Minsk, 300,000 Soviet soldiers were trapped. By August 7, von Bock's Army Group center had captured 850,000 prisoners. On October 7, the trap closed on 650,000 Russian soldiers at Vyazma near Moscow. By the end of the year twelve pockets, large and small, had been encircled in western Russia and the Ukraine. German soldiers watched as vast columns of Russian prisoners plodded westward after they had been flushed out of the woods, fields, and ruined cities. By December 1941 the Germans had taken 3,350,639 prisoners aside from casualties they had inflicted on the Soviet army. No country, they reasoned, could survive such heavy losses.

▲ Having come under sniper fire, lightly equipped German infantry approach a Russian village cautiously using the drainage ditches for cover.

A *Signal* cover and photograph show shocked and wounded Soviet prisoners. Images like this reinforced the idea that the Soviets were *Untermenschen* (Subhumans) who were ripe for defeat and enslavement.

By July 9, the German and Axis advance had crossed the old 1939 Russo-Polish border, swallowed up Latvia, Lithuania, and most of Estonia on the Baltic, and captured Minsk. By the end of September the German armies had surrounded Leningrad, the second city of the Soviet Union, Odessa on the Black Sea, and Sevastopol in the Crimea, and held a line that ran almost due south from Lake Ladoga to the Sea of Azov.

▲ A *Signal* cover features a picture story within the magazine about the crew of a PzKpfw III. The NCO commander looks out of the side hatch and leads a column of tanks (right).

▲ With a sandwich between his teeth a crewman carries two fuel cans back to the tank. The pressed steel containers universally known as "Jerricans" by the Allies were much prized as booty and copied as "AmeriCans" for the U.S. Army.

Now all that remained was a final push to capture Moscow and in Hitler's words at the beginning of Operation Barbarossa, to watch as "the whole rotten structure will come crashing down." The thrust finally came to an exhausted halt on December 5 on a line that actually was to the east of Moscow. The tanks of General Guderian's II *Panzer Armee* were at Mikhaylov about 150 kilometers south and 30 kilometers east of the Soviet capital. To the north of the city the tanks of General Erich Höppner's IV *Panzer Gruppe* had reached the outer trams stops for Moscow before they were halted by the 20th Army and 33rd Armies of the Soviet Western Front. On December 8, as winter set in, the German commanders realized that they must go onto the defensive.

Three faces of the *blitzkrieg*—motorcycle reconnaissance troops at the front, followed by an armored column, with horsedrawn logistics vehicles at the rear. A Fieseler Fi 156C-3 *Storch* (Stork) army cooperation and liaison aircraft circles the tank column looking for a safe place to land.

◄ A *Signal* cover shows a 3.7 cm Flak 37 engaging a Polikarpov fighter on an airfield near Nova-Mirapol. The Flak 37 had a horizontal range of 6,490 meters and vertical of 4,785.

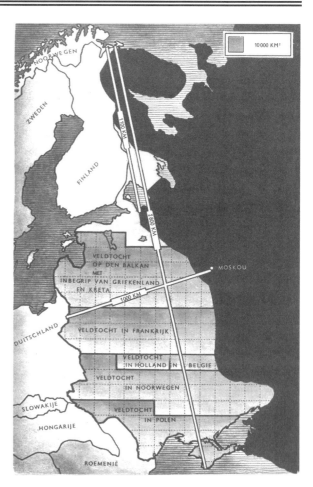

▲ A map/diagram from the Dutch language edition of *Signal* shows readers in graphic form the comparitive area and distances of Belorussia and the Ukraine compared to the Balkans and Western Europe—areas over which the Wehrmacht had already fought.

▲ *Waffen-SS* troops slump exhausted as the pace of the eastern drive begins to tell. Fatigue has often been overlooked as a factor in military plans. The huge area and vast distances in Russia, as illustrated in the map, were overwhelming for soldiers who had grown up in German cities.

On December 6, the Red Army under General Georgi Zhukov, who had already galvanized the defenses of Leningrad, launched the counterattack at Moscow. It had received fresh troops from the garrisons covering the border with Japanese controlled Manchuria, since the spy Richard Sorge based in Tokyo had informed Moscow that Japan did not intend to attack the USSR.

The Soviet counterattack was ambitious with attacks along a wide front by the North-Western Front, Kalinin Front, Western Front, and South-Western Front forces, and between January 18–22 an airborne landing by the 21st Parachute Brigade and 250th

▲ An MG 34 crew, with a 3.7 Pak 35/36 in support, prepares to leave its trenches.

◄ German gunners bring a 21 cm Mörser 18 into action. This heavy gun had a 360° traverse on its platform and could fire a 113 or 121.4 kg shell every minute out to 18,700 meters.

▼ The tension of a house to house search in a Russian village is captured in this photograph.

Airborne Regiment to the rear of the forces of German Army Group Center facing Moscow.

The fighting lasted from December to March and in that time the German forces pulled back in some sectors as much as 500 kilometers. Hitler sacked General von Brauchitsch, the army commander in chief, took command of the army, and ordered it to stand and fight. Two pockets to the north at Demyansk and Kholm held out, were supplied by air, and were later relieved by the XVI Army. The successful defense of these small pockets and the "stand and fight" order that actually prevented the collapse

▼ Engineers manhandle a *Bröckengerät* C timber and light aluminum pontoon unit in Rostov. Speedy bridging techniques enabled the Germans to gain lodgement on the eastern bank of the Don River.

▲ From behind the cover of a captured Soviet barricade German troops in Rostov await orders to advance. From on top of the barricade an MG 34 machine gun crew covers down the road.

▼ The three man crew of a 3.7 cm Pak (Sf) *auf Infanterie Schlepper,* a former French tracked infantry carrier fitted with an antitank gun, gives close support in street fighting in the city of Rostov.

▲ An MG 34 crew covers across the still waters of the Don River in Rostov. Though an excellent weapon the MG 34 was complex and would be replaced by the MG 42 later in the war.

◄ A *Signal* photograph shows a 10.5 cm *leichte Feldhaubitze* 18 that has been wheeled up to the barricade to fire its 14.81 kg shell point blank at a Soviet strong point.

of Army Group Center would be seen as a panacea by Hitler for all subsequent battles of encirclement, notably the 6th Army at Stalingrad a year later.

In spring, on May 8, 1942, the Germans launched their new offensive *Unternehmen Blau* (Operation Blue). In savage fighting at Kharkov between May 12 and 28 they defeated a Soviet offensive and then rolled eastward. The Black Sea naval base of Sevastopol fell on July 2, Rostov on the Don on July 23, and in the hot summer months the 6th Army, part of Army Group A

◄ The cover of the German army magazine *Die Wehrmacht* shows a highly decorated infantry officer at the same barricade in Rostov.

under List, reached Stalingrad on the Volga on August 24. For many of the Ukrainians and Don Cossacks the German forces were seen as liberators from the repressive government of Josef Stalin. But despite protests from some Nazi leaders the conquering forces were by design or neglect as brutal to the population as Stalin's agents. Only later were attempts made to recruit men from the Soviet Union and they would be featured in *Signal* loosely described as "Cossacks" in service with the Wehrmacht.

To the south the summer offensive reached its furthest limits on November 18. It reached the burning oil wells of Maikop by August 9 and then was into the Caucasus and within 70 miles of Grozny. The German forces were conquering territory, but were no longer rounding up huge numbers of prisoners. German *Gebirgsjäger* (mountain troops), accompanied by a film crew, even climbed the 5,641 meter high Mount El'brus in the

In a special issue *Signal* featured the "Cossacks," Russians and Ukrainians, some former prisoners, who had volunteered to fight for the Wehrmacht. Here men equipped with the German Kar 98 K rifle take cover during an exercise in a training area in eastern Europe.

▲ A horseback patrol of Cossacks wearing their distinctive black and red astrakhan *papacha* caps. The Cossacks did not wear spurs and used instead a whip or *nagaika*.

◄ The face of the *Landser*—an exhausted MG 34 gunner balances the 11.5 kg gun on his shoulder.

▶ Cossacks armed with captured Soviet weapons—the Tokarev SVT-38 automatic rifles and PPSh-41 submachine guns and 45mm PTP obr antitank gun. In the *Ost* (East) issue of *Signal* the cover (below) shows a Cossack and former Soviet political prisoner indicating where he carved his name on a prison wall.

Caucasus, and planted the swastika on the highest mountain in Europe.

Signal in 1942 could feature a map of Europe and North Africa with only Sweden, Spain, Portugal, and Switzerland, and of course Britain not colored red as either an ally or a conquest of the Third Reich. It was a powerful and beguiling image, but it was soon to change.

In Stalingrad the German forces lost the advantage of mobility and firepower as they became bogged down in grinding street fighting. Territorial gains were measured in streets, buildings, and even rooms. But the capture of

▸ Men of the 1st *Panzer Armee* look at the snowcovered peaks of the Caucasus, September 1942. The mountains traditionally known as "the mountains of the moon" were a dramatic contrast to the flat lands of the Ukraine.

Stalingrad would give the Germans control of the Volga, access to Astrakhan and the supply of petroleum from the south.

The city was held by a tough Soviet commander, General Vasili Chuikov, but by November 18, 1942, the men of his 62nd Army only held toe holds on the west bank including the Tractor,

▲ A vehicle patrol in Krupp. 1-ton trucks meet a mounted patrol in the foot hills of the Caucasus. By November 18, 1942, the German army had reached the most southern and eastern extremities of its conquests.

▸ An infantry patrol edges towards the burning installations at Maikop, captured on August 9, 1942.

Barrikady, and *Krasny Oktyabr* Factories. They had been bombed and shelled and discipline imposed by the NKVD secret police units had been ruthless to keep them in the front line. The best of the German forces were now entangled in Stalingrad and on their northern flank on the Don River bend the front lines were held by less well-equipped and trained Romanian and Italian troops. With the onset of winter, due to poor administration the 6th Army did not receive cold weather uniforms.

On November 19 Zhukov launched Operation *Uranus*. He had built up a formidable force of one million men, 13,500 guns and 894 tanks opposite the Romanian 3rd Army and Italian 8th Armies. The Soviet forces designated the South-West Front, under command of General Nikolai Vatutin and consisting of the 63rd Army, 1st Guards Army, and 21st Army, tore through the Axis forces. In five days their T-34 tanks linked up with men of the 51st Army south of Stalingrad and the trap had closed on the German 6th Army.

▲ A dramatic image for *Signal* as infantry race across the walkway of a oil loading facility in the goods yards at Maikop. Like so much of the industrial plant they were forced to relinquish, the Soviet forces had torched or demolished the wells and plant at Maikop rendering it useless for the Germans.

▲ In the suburbs of Stalingrad an MG 34 crew covers a road. Most of the wooden houses around Stalingrad were burned or destroyed in the fighting, leaving only their brick chimneys like headstones in the ashes.

◀ A *Waffen-SS* machine-gun crew swings their weapon from its AA mount against a ground target. The brutal reputation of the *Waffen-SS* in the Soviet Union meant that many did not survive capture in the long campaign.

◄ Men of the 6th Army dug in on the side of a gully on the approaches to Stalingrad. They have not yet become drawn into the harsh street fighting in the industrial city that would destroy them.

Hitler insisted that the 6th Army make no attempt to break out from Stalingrad. Göring assured Hitler that the *Luftwaffe* could supply the trapped army but it was a promise that was beyond the capability of the *Luftwaffe*. They did manage to fly out some casualties and bring in supplies, but intense antiaircraft fire and long flights made it an increasingly hazardous journey. On the ground Field Marshal von Manstein, commanding the 4th *Panzer Armee*, was ordered to break into the encirclement and attempted this between December 12 and 23. If the 6th Army had been allowed to attempt a break out to meet him they might have saved many lives. The Russians halted the relief attempt and kept

▲ A soldier prepares to throw a stick grenade in this striking *Signal* cover. Though Moscow in 1941–42 had been a set back, *Signal* presented an optimistic coverage of the summer campaign of 1942. The Germans with their allies were capturing huge areas and Stalingrad appeared about to fall.

▶ A Stuka's eye view of Stalingrad in this vertigo inducing photograph of an attack on the railway yards. The Soviet forces realized that if they kept as close as possible to the German front line, enemy dive-bombers and artillery were less effective since they risked hitting their own troops.

▲ A standard bearer of the Spanish Division *Azul,* the Spanish volunteer force, so named because of the color of their Falangist shirts, arrived in Eastern Europe for deployment in Russia. Some 47,000 Spaniards fought in the Division Azul. *Signal* made much of these volunteers against Bolshevism.

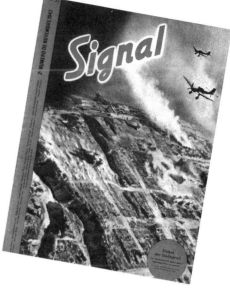

Signal featured the Stukas and He III bombers of the *Luftwaffe's* VIII Air Corps as they pounded Stalingrad.

▼ A captured Soviet 37 mm AA gun, one of the many that would make air operations over Stalingrad increasingly hazardous.

up the pressure. Day by day they closed in on the working airfields and finally had them within artillery range.

On Christmas Day the Propaganda Ministry of Dr. Joseph Goebbels broadcast Christmas greetings from the crew of a U-boat in the Atlantic, men of the *Afrika Korps* in North Africa, the garrison of the Atlantic Wall defenses, and over a crackling radio link, the men of Stalingrad, "the front on the Volga." Their

▲ In the dust and smoke of street fighting an NCO in charge of an MG 34 crew holds a 9 mm Pistole 08, the pistol universally known as the Luger.

▲ In relative safety a German officer, with a cloth helmet cover, still needs to watch the roof tops for snipers in Stalingrad.

▲ A *Storch* eye view of a small convoy in a Russian village forms the cover of *Die Wehrmacht.*

voices then blended together in *Stille Nacht,* the classic German Christmas carol. It was dramatic and very moving—and faked in radio studios in Berlin.

On January 13, 1943, the recently promoted Field Marshal Paulus surrendered. Figures for Stalingrad are hard to establish but German and Axis losses were in the region of 1.5 million men, 3,500 tanks, 12,000 guns and mortars, 75,000 vehicles, and 3,000 aircraft.

At Moscow in the winter of 1941–42 Nazi Germany was fated not to win World War II, at Stalingrad a year later it was doomed to lose it.

◄ The commander of a column of 7.5 cm StuG III Ausf F assault guns gazes at the photographer over the top of the artillery scissors periscope. Assault guns could provide direct fire for tanks and Panzer Grenadiers and were increasingly used as antitank vehicles.

▼ Henschel Hs 123A-1 ground-attack aircraft on a snowcovered Russian airfield. Despite its archaic appearance the Hs 123 proved a tough and effective ground-attack aircraft with a bomb load of 450 kg and two 20 mm cannon.

SIGNAL—THE WORLD'S FIRST COLOR SUPPLEMENT

A S A BIMONTHLY SPECIAL edition of the *Berliner Illustrierte Zeitung (The Berlin Illustrated News)*, *Signal* with its color pages was effectively the world's first newspaper color supplement.

The magazine was 36 x 27 mm and in 1940 had 46 pages, though paper shortages reduced this during the war. The excellent technical quality of the magazine was the responsibility of Franz Hugo Mässlang. Contributors included Heinrich Hunke, Walter Kiaulehn, Walter Grüvell, Kurt Zentner, and Alfred Ernst Johann.

In a red strap running along the left hand side of the cover were the prices for the different national editions, with the month and date. At the top was the number of the issue and the language it was produced in, so a French edition might be for example F No 13 and a Spanish edition Sp No 15. The caption for the cover picture was in a red disc at the bottom right. The German national colors of red, black, and white dominated layouts and maps.

The first half of the magazine had news stories. These were often a picture story or used artist's impressions, maps, or diagrams. The second half covered domestic news and features about the arts and entertainment industry. The eight color pages reflected this editorial balance.

Signal carried advertisements for armaments side by side with those for domestic manufacturers like Adler, Agfa, Mercedes-Benz, Deutsche Bank, Olympia, Zeiss, and even the German State Lottery—*Der Deutsche Reichslotterie*.

Advertisements and domestic photographs in *Signal* were sometimes a startling contrast to pictures showing the harsh realities of war such as this NCO armed with a MP38/40 during fighting in central Russia in the autumn of 1941. ▶

▲ Using a large pneumatic assault boat German soldiers cross a small river in France in May 1940. The use of these assault boats by German pioneers enabled them to construct improvised bridges, rafts, and ferries before larger bridges were built.

▶ A French shell bursts on a railway embankment as a machine gun section takes cover. In May 1940 the Germans were surprised how French artillery fire was so ill-coordinated—in World War I it had been awesome.

▶ The MG 34 crew have set up the machine gun on its Lafette 34 sustained fire mount with optical sight, it gave greater stability and allowed the gun to engage targets at 2,000 meters.

▲ PzKpfw 38(t) and PzKpfw II tanks advance through the woodland of a French country estate in May 1940. Though lightly armored in comparison to some French and British tanks, these light vehicles were handled with greater tactical skill and exploited the weaknesses and gaps in the French defenses.

◀ One of the most enduring images in *Signal,* a German tank commander in his PzKpfw IV Ausf B or C. He is wearing the black panzer uniform with death's head collar insignia with rose pink piping (*waffenfarbe*) and the *Schutzmütze* beret over his padded crash helmet.

◀ A pioneer in action with a *Flammenwerfer* 35, the flame thrower had a single trigger that operated the pressurized nitrogen tank and ignited the oil fuel.

▼ With water bottles, mess tins, and mail, a soldier returns to his section in the front line.

▶ German trucks bring infantry forward to positions near the Somme River during the battle of France in June 1940. Though the French fought hard, by now the German forces were superior in numbers as well as weapons, equipment, and armored tactics.

▲ PzKpfw I tanks push through the burned and blasted remains of a village in northern France. Fast moving armored columns appearing unexpectedly to the rear of positions paralyzed the planners in French headquarters.

◄ Wearing the M1915 steel helmet, General Kurt von Briesen takes the salute of a motorized column as it moves through a tree-lined boulevard in central Paris.

◀ Photographed for *Signal* by the rear gunner of another Messerschmitt Bf 110C-4, a German fighter patrols along the chalk cliffs of southern England—or more likely northern France. In the battle of Britain eight Gruppen of Bf110Cs and Ds took part in the campaign but suffered heavy losses.

◀ A Messerschmitt Bf 109 closes on a Supermarine Spitfire 1A—the picture appeared in *Signal* as a double page spread giving the impression that the air campaign over Britain was going well. However as losses mounted *Luftwaffe* air crew saw that the RAF were a formidable opponent.

▲ In early September *Luftwaffe* fighter pilots rest on an airfield in northern France while their Bf 109s wait ready for takeoff. With their deck chairs and the roughly camouflaged bell tent their appearance is almost identical to that of the RAF across the Channel.

◀ Ground crew ready an He III of III *Gruppe Kampfgeschwader* 26 "Löwen." Based in Norway the bomber group attacked targets in northern England and Scotland. For the crews of damaged aircraft there was a nervewracking return flight across the North Sea.

◀ Mussolini and General Jodl study a battle plan with Hitler in the map room of his Eastern Front headquarters as Field Marshal Keitel looks on.

▼ Ground crew warm the engines of a Fiat BR.20M bomber on an airfield in Belgium. *Signal* featured these aircraft, though only small numbers were used in the battle of Britain.

▲ General Erwin Rommel confers with his staff at Sollum. They wear new *Afrika Korps* tropical issue uniforms in sage green. Uniforms made in this color and in sand tan bleached out quickly in the harsh sunlight of North Africa.

▼ Dust swirls around an airfield in Libya with Bf 110 and Ju 52s. Axis airfields became a target for raids by the SAS who destroyed the valuable transport aircraft crucial for the supply of reinforcements and spares.

▲ Dressed in their issue sun helmets, an MG34 crew in a rocky position in the Aegean. Field emplacements constructed from rocks while strong, had the drawback that fragments of stone could cause secondary injuries, particularly to the face and upper body.

▶ *Signal's* dramatic picture of a BMW R75 crew as they roar through the dust. The markings on the sidecar show that they are from 3rd Battery Field Artillery 21 Panzer Division and the men have the distinctive red *Waffenfarbe* piping of the artillery on their caps.

▶ A PzKpfw IV passes an abandoned British tracked Universal Carrier in North Africa. A small number of these captured vehicles were converted into self-propelled antitank guns with a 3.7 cm Pak mounted on the engine behind the driver's compartment.

▼ During a ceremonial parade a *Luftwaffe* standard bearer presents the colors in front of a Bf109 (Trop) of I *Gruppe Jagdgeschwader* 27. For the parade he wears jack boots, the metal gorget, and carrying sash for the colors.

▲ In a *Signal* picture that appears distinctly contrived— no one would stand close to a burning combat aircraft— German airborne forces examine a USAAF Lockheed P-38 Lightning shot down in Tunisia. Coverage of the U.S. forces by *Signal* was initially patronizing as they were not a "real enemy."

▶ The commander of an SdKfz 250/3 of 3rd Battery 21 Panzer Division holds onto the frame antenna as the vehicle bucks through the sand towards the *Signal* photographer. The war in the desert, though harsh, had none of the politicized brutality of the war in Russia.

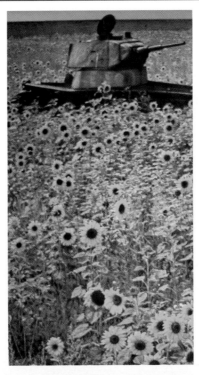

◀ A striking *Signal* image of a knocked out Soviet T-26S tank in a field of sunflowers. The T-26S, known to the Germans as the T-26C, had a crew of three and was armed with a 45 mm gun and co-axial 7.62 mm DT MG machine gun.

▲ Men of the *Waffen-SS* cavalry division *Florian Geyer* near Minsk in 1941 during the advance into Russia. Mottled camouflaged smocks and helmet covers were initially a *Waffen-SS* distinction.

▼ *Signal* showed these bogged down T-34/76 tanks near Tolotshin on the Drut as an example of the poor training of the Soviet army. The tank with its well angled armor and powerful M1940 76.2 mm gun was a nasty shock for the invading Germans forces and their allies.

▼ A swastika flag is spread out to show the position of the German front line to *Luftwaffe* ground attack aircraft in Russia in 1942.

▲ A *Luftwaffe* Flak artillery officer cuts a souvenir from a downed Soviet fighter. The officer has the distinctive red Flak colors on his collar rank insignia.

◀ A dispatch rider slumps exhausted over his battered Zündapp 597 cc KS600 motorcycle. The poor roads in Russia punished men and machines as the Germans pushed eastwards and further away from their logistic bases and workshops.

▶ A coup for *Signal* on the cover of the Dutch edition. Stalin's son Vasili was captured in 1941 and disowned by his father.

▲ Smoke pours from a knocked out Soviet vehicle that has been engaged by a 3.7 cm Pak 35/36. The Pak 35/36 was no threat to the T-34 and the tough Soviet tank was only stopped by the formidable 8.8 cm Flak gun firing solid shot.

▶ Casualties begin to mount in Russia and these German graves marked by the arrow shaped non-Christian tir rune probably belong to men of the *Waffen-SS*. Interest in runes, an ancient form of writing grew with German nationalism in the 19th Century. The SS collar insignia was a runic device.

◀ Ju 87 Stukas move into the line abreast formation that precedes an attack. On the Eastern Front Stukas were still effective in ground attack in 1943 and saw action at Kursk.

▼ A *Waffen-SS* officer, armed with an MP38/40 submachine gun, watches the crew of a Soviet T-34 as they dismount to surrender.

▶ A PzKpfw III thunders across the burning steppe in the opening phases of Operation *Zitadelle* near the Kursk salient in July 1943. *Signal* showed photographs of tanks in action and Soviet prisoners but the operation was a disaster and marked the beginning of the end for German forces in Russia.

▲ The strength of the Atlantic Wall was exaggerated by this striking *Signal* picture of the 40.6 cm SK C/34 guns of the *Batterie Lindemann* at the Pas de Calaise.

Women who had been told by the Nazis that their place was in the home bringing up children were now the heroines of *Signal* in the battle for production. The cover shows a woman checking off an aircraft engine of a Bf 109 on a production line shown above.

THE ROAD TO DEFEAT 1943–1945

"It is not sufficient to give clear and tactically correct orders. All officers and men of the Army, the Air Force and the Naval forces must be penetrated by a fanatical will to end the battle victoriously, and never to relax until the last enemy soldier has been destroyed or thrown back into the sea. The battle must be fought in a spirit of holy hatred."

—Teleprinter signal from Hitler to Field Marshal Kesselring
28 January 1944

NORTH AFRICA AND THE MEDITERRANEAN

T he second battle of Alamein began on the night of October 23, 1942. It soon became a grim slogging match as the superior forces of the British and Commonwealth 8th Army under General Bernard Montgomery attempted to break through the thick defenses of the Axis position. With superior numbers Montgomery was able to switch his attacks between the north and south, but it was not until November 4, when his tank force had been reduced to 30, that Rommel was forced to retreat. Montgomery did not press the *Afrika Korps* as it withdrew, despite detailed ULTRA information about its weakened state.

▼ The map and inset photograph from *Signal* show how tantalizingly close Rommel and the *Afrika Korps* came to capturing Egypt and the strategic Suez Canal. Maps in *Signal* ranged from the strictly tactical through political to the pictorial.

Generalfeldmarschall Rommel mit seinem Stab während der Kämpfe in Nordafrika

▲ Erwin Rommel, nicknamed the Desert Fox, outfought and outwitted British and Commonwealth generals for nearly three years in North Africa. He is shown on this French language edition of *Signal*.

▲ An oil drum sign post at the end of the coastal railroad track. Manmade landmarks were vital for navigation. Dehydration and heat were a problem, as were flash floods and low temperatures at night.

▼ The Tobruk antitank ditch bridged by the Germans after the capture of the port. They were unable to hold it and withdrew after the defeat at El Alamein.

▲ An *Afrika Korps* officer checks his watch prior to the assault on the South African held port of Tobruk. Taking Tobruk and the battle of Kasserine would be Rommel's last victories in World War II.

▲ Smoke rises from trucks machine-gunned by tanks in the chaos of a fast moving mechanized battle in the desert.

On November 8 the Anglo-American *Torch* landings took place at Morocco and Algeria and the Germans and Italians were caught between two armies. On November 9, the Germans quickly flew reinforcements into Tunisia from Sicily. With fresh troops, new equipment, and inspired leadership the Germans held out until May 11, 1943, and on February 19 in his final throw in North Africa Rommel would defeat U.S. forces at Kasserine Pass. *Signal* featured the shocked and tired faces of U.S. soldiers as they were marched into captivity. Following this success on

◀ Rommel in his Sd Kfz 250/3 half track with its distinctive red and white lettered name *Greif.* Rommel used a variety of armored and soft skin vehicles to lead from the front in the fighting in North Africa. He was always at a disadvantage since ULTRA intercepts of his signals allowed 8th Army commanders to second guess his moves.

▶ American GIs plod disconsolately to the rear after the defeat at Kasserine. *Signal* made much of this local victory but the strategic situation was moving against the Axis with America's entry into the war.

▸ A gutted 8th Army Lee/Grant tank—though designed and built in the United States, these tanks reflected the combat experience of the British tank commission that visited the U.S. in June 1940. Construction began in August 1941 and ended in December 1942 by which time a total of 6,258 had been built.

◂ *Afrika Korps* soldiers examine a knocked out M3A5 Lee/Grant tank supplied to the 8th Army from the United States. The tank had a crew of seven and its powerful 75 mm hull mounted gun was able to destroy Axis armor at long range while the turret mounted 37 mm gun could be used against secondary targets.

March 9, Rommel was replaced by General von Arnim as commander-in-chief of the Axis forces. If the "Desert Fox" had been obliged to surrender, German morale, somewhat battered, would have been badly hurt. A few hundred soldiers escaped by air to Sicily but over 150,000 were taken prisoner. It was the end of the *Afrika Korps*.

The next move by the Allies seemed obvious—an attack on Sicily, the mainland territory of the Fascist adversary. Churchill urged it, describing Italy as "the soft underbelly" of the Third Reich. In fact it was remarkably tough and the fighting lasted from July 9, 1943, to May 2, 1945. Even as the Allies pushed up the Italian peninsula *Signal* not only gave an accurate record of the fighting withdrawal, but was even able to feature local successes and victories.

▲ *Signal* ran a picture story on the USAAF pilot of the P-38F fighter and the *Luftwaffe* pilot who shot him down, clearly a combat veteran who had been decorated with the Knight's Cross.

▶ In their distinctive color scheme of black with a white cross, water containers are topped up. A *Signal* photo feature followed a water container in the course of a day—among the many people who used it was a captured British soldier.

▲ Cannon fire from a Bf 109 rips apart an aircraft of the RAF Desert Air Force. By 1943 most ground attack operations in North Africa were undertaken by the USAAF and RAF.

▼ Grim faced men of the *Afrika Korps* march into captivity in this Allied photograph. Though some had escaped from Tunisia back to Sicily the bulk were forced to surrender to the Anglo-American forces in Tunisia.

The weight of the defense of Italy fell on the capable shoulders of Albert Kesselring, a *Luftwaffe* Field Marshal who became an able land commander. Born in Bavaria in 1885 he joined the army and served on the Western Front in World War I. In 1936 he was made chief of the general staff of the *Luftwaffe*. Under his command *Luftflotte I* supported the army in 1939 in Poland and 1940 in Flanders.

From December 1941 to March 1945, Kesselring was commander in chief of the armed forces in the Mediterranean area (Italy and North Africa). Under his command the Germans fought a series of actions on defense lines across the Italian peninsula. From March 25 to May 6, 1945, Kesselring was responsible for combat operations in western Germany. He introduced himself to the staff of his demoralized HQ staff in Germany with

▼ A ground crew works around a Bf 109 in its dispersal bay. The neatly banked soil protects the fighter from bomb fragments and cannon fire, while the trench allows the *Luftwaffe* personnel to take cover. The Bf 109 was the fighter in which Hauptman Hans-Joachim Marseille, flying with Jg 52 and 27, scored 151 victories in North Africa.

a broad grin and the words, "Good morning gentlemen, I am the new V3." His optimism in some tough and difficult situations earned him the nickname "Smiling Al."

On the night of July 9-10, 1943, British and American airborne forces landed on Sicily. They were the advanced guard for the U.S. 5th Army and British 8th Army. The American forces landed on the southern coast and advanced northwest to take Palermo on July 22 and then turned east to clear the island. On July 11–12 the Herman Göring Panzer Division launched a counterattack against the American 1st Infantry Division at Gela that actually reached the coastal dunes before it was broken up by naval gunfire. The British landed on the southeast tip and advanced north toward Messina. The German forces put up a strong resistance and their demolitions and rearguard actions

▲ Field Marshal Albert Kesselring returns a salute with his baton. A former artillery officer in World War I he proved an able *Luftwaffe* officer. He then commanded ground troops fighting a series of delaying actions on defensive lines in Italy, notably at Monte Cassino, and also managed to bottle up the Allied landings at Salerno and Anzio.

◀ *Signal* had a victory to celebrate when German forces launched a successful airborne and amphibious operation in October 1943 against the Aegean islands of Kos and Leros held by an Anglo-Italian force. German losses were 12 merchant ships and 20 landing craft sunk and 4,000 men drowned.

▼ A map in *Signal* showing the landing and the withdrawal through Sicily was an attempt to put a positive gloss on what was the first loss of Axis territory. The Germans slowed the advance by demolitions, nuisance minefields, and ambushes, but the outcome was inevitable.

▸ After the event *Signal* ran a feature on the Allied invasion and the fighting withdrawal through Sicily to the Straits of Messina. The phase lines marked on the map give the impression of a controlled operation, but in reality the German and Italian troops were under constant pressure.

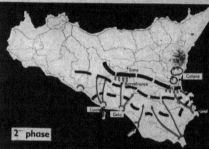

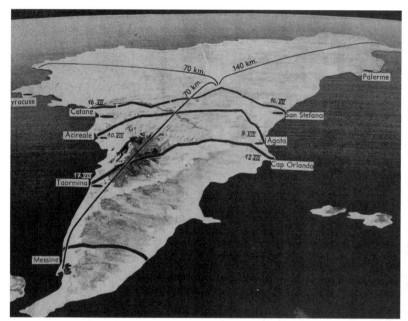

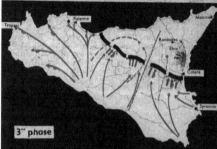

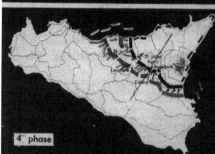

meant that Messina did not fall until August 17, 1943. Prior to its capture, the German and Italian naval forces evacuated 40,000 German troops, 60,000 Italian troops, nearly 10,000 German vehicles, and 47 tanks across the Straits of Messina to the Italian mainland.

Secret negotiations between the Allies and Italy had confirmed that the Italians wanted to surrender and planned to arrest Mussolini in July. On September 3, the 8th Army crossed the Straits of Messina in Operation *Baytown*. On September 9, hours before the Italians announced their surrender, the British 1st Airborne Division landed at Brindisi and in Operation *Avalanche* the U.S. 6th Corps and British 10th Corps landed at Salerno as a jumping-off point for the capture of the city of Naples. With Italy's withdrawal from the war they assumed that the landings would be unopposed.

But the Germans had made an assessment of likely beachheads

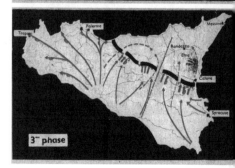

◄ A Pz Kpfw V Ausf D Panther drives through Rome. The Panther drew on the lessons of the Eastern Front and with its 7.5 cm KwK K.42 gun was a highly effective tank. The Germans reacted very quickly to the news of Italy's surrender and drove quickly down through the peninsula to intercept the Allied landings and disarm Italian troops.

▲ A U.S. army Jeep and M10 Tank Destroyer smashed by artillery fire in 1943 in southern Italy. The PK photographer who took this picture would have delighted the *Signal* staff with this image, albeit small, of a German victory.

and reacted quickly to the Salerno landings. Two Panzer Divisions put the Anglo-American force under such pressure that there was some consideration about evacuating the coastal position. In the end the 8th Army advancing from the south forced the Germans to retire to the Gustav Line. Naples was liberated on October 1, 1943.

Mussolini who had been ordered to resign as leader of Italy by King Victor Emmanuel III, the Fascist Grand Council, and Marshal Badoglio, was arrested and held in a secret location. By ingenious signals intercepts the Germans were able to find his prison, a remote winter sports hotel in the Apennines called Gran Sasso. Since the hotel could only be reached by a funicular railway, an airborne assault was the only viable rescue option. On September 12, 1943, paratroops of the 1st Company of the

◄ An officer heads a column of British and American prisoners, captured at Anzio in 1944. Hitler was determined to destroy the beach head north of Monte Casino.

▲ *Fallschirmjäger*. Though trained as airborne forces, after Crete they were employed as ground troops on all fronts.

▲ PzKpfw V Ausf D Panthers in Italy, later models had 5 mm side plates and Zimmerit antimagnetic mine coating. The subsequent Ausf A and G models had a hull-mounted machine gun.

▶ *Gebirgsjäger* (mountain troops) armed with an MG 34 machine gun prepare to engage Allied aircraft in a position in the Gustav Line.

◀ A *Signal* photographer covered the hazardous departure of Mussolini and Skorzeny in a *Fieseler Storch*. The paratroops and *Waffen-SS* men held the aircraft until it had developed sufficient power for it to clear the drop at the end of the improvised air strip at Gran Sasso.

Un communiqué historique:
La libération de Mussolini

Fallschirmjäger Lehrbataillon, commanded by Lieutenant von Berlepsch, and a small group of *Waffen-SS* men commanded by *Obersturmbannführer* Otto Skorzeny, lifted off in twelve DFS 230 gliders. Eight of the gliders reached the rocky landing zone by the hotel and Mussolini was rescued with no casualties. Paratroops had seized the funicular railway, but Skorzeny and Mussolini made their exit in a hazardous flight in a Fieseler *Storch* observation and liaison aircraft. For *Signal* this was a dramatic "good news" story. A separate supplement was produced and later color photographs were published of the *Storch* taking off from its rocky airstrip.

▲ The *Signal* special supplement that appeared inside the September 1943 French language issue of the magazine. It had dramatic, but not inaccurate illustrations of the German raid that liberated Mussolini from the mountain hotel. The face of his rescuer, Otto Skorzeny, appears in the bottom right corner.

◄ A section of German paratroops prepares for a fighting patrol in the ruins of Monte Cassino. The defense of the of the monastery and the Gothic Line was featured in *Signal* as a picture story with a dramatic three dimensional map. Terrible weather and the stubborn bravery of the paratroops held up the Allies until the summer of 1944.

▶ An MG 42 crew in the ruins of the monastery of Monte Cassino. Their lace up rubber soled boots were more practical than jack boots or the ankle boots that were issued to soldiers from 1943.

▲ A StuG III Ausf G fuer StuK 40 L/48 assault gun in the blasted remains of Cassino town. In the latter years of the war German tank and assault gun crews became expert in making the most of very few or even single armored vehicles.

Further south the Germans withdrew to the Gustav or Winter Line that had been built in the Apennines running from the mouth of the Garigliano, through Monte Cassino, to a point south of Ortona. The line was held by 15 divisions of the German 10th Army. The battle for the Gustav Line and its key position of the sixth-century mountain top Benedictine monastery of Monte Cassino became an epic of endurance by the German para-troopers *Fallschirmjäger* who held the position. It was attacked by the British X Corps, American II Corps, and the French Corps from January 17 to February 12, 1944. The monastery was bombed on February 15, but the paratroopers hung on when the 4th Indian Division and 2nd New Zealand Division captured the town but were ejected in a counterattack. The Germans made

◀ In a forward observation post a paratrooper scans the dust and smoke above Cassino town. He has an MG 42 and MP 40 close to hand and a stick grenade rests on the parapet of his position.

▲ Resting on a grenade box, a paratrooper takes aim with the unique *Fallschirmjägergewehr* 42. This weapon fired a full-sized 7.92 mm x 57 rifle cartridge from a twenty round magazine and had a cyclic rate of 750 rounds per minute. About 7,000 guns were delivered by 1945.

considerable propaganda mileage out of the destruction of the monastery and had taken the precaution of removing the art treasures. Once the building had been reduced to ruins, the paratroops moved in and fortified them. Their stubborn defense earned them a unique tribute from Hitler who asserted that they were harder than the *Waffen-SS*.

Kesselring's tactical genius was amply demonstrated when in an attempt to outflank the Gustav Line the American 3rd and British 1st Infantry Divisions landed at Anzio, a port on the western coast of Italy on January 22, 1944. Initially they achieved complete surprise but Kesselring reacted quickly calling down the *Fallschirmjäger Korps* and 76th Corps held in reserve near Rome. He did not have to withdraw troops from the Gustav Line,

▶ The strain shows on the faces of paratroops in this *Signal* photograph. The distinctive rimless *Fallschirmjäger* helmet can be seen as well as the practical jump smock. The camouflaged smock came to midthigh and had deep pockets with zip closures. They have the standard Zeiss 6 x 30 prismatic Dienstglas, the binoculars widely issued to German ground troops down to the NCO commanding a machine gun section. German optical equipment was of a very high standard and was widely prized booty for Allied soldiers.

▲ The PzKpfw VI Tiger with its 8.8 cm gun featured on the cover of the Spanish language *Signal* was a potent symbol of German technological advance.

and Hitler urged him to destroy the beachhead supplying reinforcements. The beachhead at Anzio was effectively under siege until May 23, 1944, when Allied troops broke through the Gustav Line.

The final battle for the Gustav Line, Operation *Diadem*, saw 2,000 guns bombarding the German positions. The Polish II Corps isolated the monastery as the British crossed the Liri River west of Cassino to cut Route 6 west of the town, and the American and French Corps attacked south of the river. The four month battle for the Monte Cassino position had cost the Allies 21,000 casualties including 4,100 killed, German losses were comparable.

▸ Pioneers dig up a street in Florence to position T.Mi.42 Tellermine antitank mines. All the bridges across the Arno, with the exception of the Ponte Veccio, were blown up and the wreckage mined to impede the Allied advance.

A combination of Kesselring's tactical skill and the U.S. General Mark Clark's ambition to see the American 5th Army liberate Rome allowed the German forces to evade encirclement. They withdrew to the 16-km deep Gothic Line from Le Spezia on the west, to the Adriatic between Pesaro and Cattolica, which they had consolidated by June 16. In front of the Gothic Line were a series of temporary defensive lines that delayed the Allied advance. The Albert Line, which the 8th Army broke through on June 22, was based on Lake Trasimene and straddled the center of the peninsula. The Arno Line, which the 8th Army attacked on July 15, 1944, used the line of the Arno River and covered the western half of Italy. The Allies broke through and on August 4 liberated Florence.

On August 15 Operation *Dragoon*, the airborne and amphibious invasion of southern France, was launched, drawing off over 86,000 Franco-American forces from Italy. The German 19th Army defending the area withdrew up the Rhone valley, and in mid-September near Dijon forward patrols linked up with Allied forces who had landed at Normandy on June 6.

◀ PzKpfw IV Ausf G secured on railway flat cars. The Ausf G had a distinctive double muzzle brake on its KwK 40 L/43 gun and 30 mm side armor. The Germans had few road transporters and favored moving tanks to the front line by rail.

▶ Across the Adriatic the Germans had been fighting a savage war with the Yugoslav Partisans commanded by the charismatic Serb leader General Tito.

▼ *Signal* in English—a cover picture of General U.S. Grant and a long article on the Anaconda strategy employed by the Union against the Confederacy in the American Civil War. It suggested that the United States would employ similar blockade tactics against Germany.

On August 25, British, Canadian, and Polish troops attacked the Gothic Line, but it was not until September 12 that the battle began in earnest. The German 10th Army fought hard but by September 24 the Allies were through the defenses. Canadian troops occupied Ravenna on December 5. Fighting slowed down with the onset of winter and on March 25, 1945 General Heinrich von Vietinghoff succeeded Kesselring as commander in chief in Italy.

The Allied spring offensive was launched on April 9. American General Mark Clark who had succeeded General Harold Alexander as the commander in chief of the 15th Army Group not only had a depleted force, but one of the most heterogeneous field armies of the war with contingents from over 25 countries. Polish forces captured Bologna on the 21st and five days later Verona and Genoa fell and with their fall German resistance collapsed.

The Salo Republic, the German puppet Italian Fascist State set up following the Allied invasion of the mainland in 1943 and headed by Mussolini, had been in northern Italy with its headquarters at Lake Garda. Now without his German allies to protect him, Mussolini attempted to escape into Switzerland hidden with his mistress Clara Petacci in a convoy of German troops. The

▲ The crew of a Ju 188E-1 medium bomber are briefed in preparation for a night intruder mission in Italy.

convoy was intercepted on April 27 by Italian partisans on the shore of Lake Como. The Germans were allowed to continue but the Italians were pulled off the trucks. Mussolini huddled in a German soldier's overcoat but was recognized, held overnight, and executed on April 28, 1945. Clara Petacci died with him trying to protect her lover from the hail of submachine-gun fire. Their bodies were hung up in a public square in Milan.

General Karl Wolff the 44-year-old military governor and SS chief in northern Italy, who had acted as the liaison officer between Hitler and Mussolini, was convinced that the war was lost. In secret meetings in Switzerland with Allen Dulles the head of intelligence at the Office of Strategic Services (OSS) (the organization that would become the CIA), Wolff negotiated the surrender of German forces in Italy.

Six days before Victory in Europe Day (VE Day) on May 2, 1945, German forces in Italy capitulated.

▲ *Signal's* pin ups and photographs evoking dreams of summer leave appealed to soldiers on both sides. From 1943 onward there were more of these beguiling images in the magazine.

RUSSIA—THE FIGHTING WITHDRAWAL

"The hard and costly struggle against Bolshevism during the last two and a half years, which has involved the bulk of our military strength in the East, has demanded extreme exertions. The greatness of the danger and the general situation demanded it."

—Adolf Hitler, *Directive No 51, November 3, 1943*

▼ A column of StuG III Ausf G assault guns of a *Waffen-SS* Panzer Division in 1943. The rear decks are cluttered with storage boxes and equipment. The tracks have been modified for operations in snow.

On February 18, 1943, following the surrender of the 6th Army at Stalingrad, Dr. Joseph Goebbels addressed a picked audience at the *Sportpalastrede* (Sports Palace) in Berlin. Under a huge banner that read *Totaler Krieg für Zester Krieg* (Total War for Shortest War), he gave a powerful speech that carried his audience with him as they pledged themselves for combat and sacrifice.

Goebbels hurled ten questions at the fanaticized crowd to which they thundered back *Ja!* The last question was "Do you want total war?" When the affirmation was roared back Goebbels replied with the words of the great call to war in 1812, "Let Our War-Cry be: Now the People Rise Up and Storm Break Loose!"

The mobilization in the name of Total War included the drafting of women into industry and air defense and by 1945 over seven and a half million were working in these fields. *Signal* featured them often on color front pages. Cultural life came to

▼ A soldier of the *Waffen-SS* takes aim with a Mauser C96 *Schnellfeuerpistole* during fighting in Russia. This weapon had the 20-round magazine and with the shoulder stock fitted had a maximum range of 300 meters.

▶ Not every cover featured martial themes—the back covers were largely devoted to glamorous domestic or romantic images which sustained a nostalgic illusion of normality for soldiers in the front line.

▲ Under international neutral supervision the bodies of murdered Polish officers are exhumed from their mass grave in the woods of Katyn in Russia. Katyn was heavily featured in all editions of *Signal* as an example of Soviet barbarity.

a halt, with the exception of entertainment that would boost the workers' morale.

On May 26, 1943, German forces discovered mass graves at a forest at Katyn near Smolensk. They contained the bodies of 4,500 Polish officers captured by the Russians in 1939. The men had been bound and shot in the back of the head by Stalin's secret police, the NKVD. For *Signal* and the Nazis this was a propaganda coup and they tried hard to exploit it to create division among the Allies. The work of a neutral commission was interrupted when German forces were forced to withdraw in September.

The high moral tone publicly adopted by the Nazis over Katyn contrasted with the secrecy that surrounded the work of *SS-Brigadeführer* Jürgen Stroop, who on April 19, 1943, led a force of 2,000 SS, army, and Eastern European troops into the Warsaw

▶ German officers confer by a Sdfz 251. The man in the foreground has a colored armband on his left sleeve. This practice was adopted by the Germans to distinguish their troops from the Russians when both sides were dressed in white winter camouflage uniforms.

Ghetto with instructions to liquidate it. By now the Polish Jews knew about the extermination camps and had determined to resist deportation, and a force of 1,500 lightly armed men and women fought until May 16. Stroop's forces captured or killed 56,065 Jews during the battle, German losses were about 400 dead and 1,000 wounded. About 50 Jewish fighters escaped through the sewers into Warsaw.

▲ This *Signal* photograph shows MG 42 machine gunners putting down covering fire. The gun could be modified for operations in extreme cold weather with the gunner wearing heavy mits or gloves.

Despite the huge losses following the surrender at Stalingrad, Hitler remained optimistic. On February 16, 1943, Kharkov fell to the advancing Soviet forces of General Filip Golikov's Voronezh Front and General Nikolai Vatutin's South-West Front. However four days later spearheaded by the *Waffen-SS*, Field Marshal Manstein's Army Group South counterattacked the southern flank of both fronts inflicting heavy losses and forcing them back behind the Donets River. By March 15, 1943, the city

▼ In a damp winter haze a StuG IV assault gun passes a machine gun crew in their shallow foxhole. The frozen soil made good going for armored vehicles, but was a nightmare for infantry attempting to dig field positions such as trenches and bunkers.

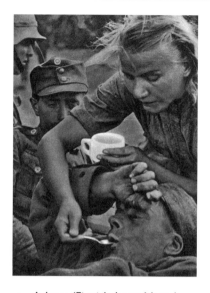

▲ A *Lotta* (Finnish Army Nurse) featured in *Signal* feeds a wounded Finnish soldier. In the canon of racial purity the Nordic nations were an ideal for the Nazis and Finns and Norwegian volunteers were often photographed.

▲ A Finnish soldier armed with a *Konepistooli* m/31 submachine gun known as a "*Suomi*" shelters in a water-logged trench. As Soviet pressure increased, Finland opted to withdraw from its alliance and turned against Germany.

was again in German hands. Part of the reason for Manstein's triumph may have been his close tactical control of the fast moving battle. There were no long encoded signals back to Hitler's HQ at Rastenburg in East Prussia. It was signals like these that were the undoing of German plans since they were intercepted and decoded as part of the ULTRA operation at Bletchley Park.

Fighting in Russia normally slowed down with the spring thaw that produced immobility as the roads turned to soft mud. After Kharkov the front line stabilized into a huge Soviet salient 190 km wide and 120 km deep that had the railway city of Kursk at its center. The German summer offensive of 1943 aimed to pinch out this bulge with attacks from the north by Army Group Center under Kluge and from the south by Army Group South under Manstein. The attacks would be code named *Unternehmen Zitadelle* (Operation Citadel).

Possibly the greatest triumph of ULTRA was the interception of the plans for Operation Citadel that were passed to the Soviet Union through the Lucy spy ring in Switzerland. This gave the Red Army a massive advantage when the Germans attacked the salient in July.

The German plan was not as ambitious as the offensives of 1941 and 1942. Hitler saw it as an operation that would give Germany psychological leverage after Stalingrad and "light a bonfire" that would impress the world and possibly intimidate the Soviet high command.

▲ A *Waffen-SS* 4 x 2 Kfz 15 churns through the mud. The vehicle started life as a British Army Morris-Commercial 8-cwt truck and was one of many captured in France in 1940. It was given German Kfz 15 bodywork and became part of the *Waffen-SS* inventory. The drawback of using captured weapons and vehicles was accessing spares and ammunition which created a major problem for workshops and logisticians.

◄ The crew of a heavily laden BMW R75 of a *Wehrmacht* Motorized Infantry Regiment struggle to move their machine on a Russian road turned glutinous in the spring thaw.

▶ A *Gebirgsjäger* officer shares a cigarette with the crew of a Pz Kpfw IV Ausf F1. The officer has the silver tank destruction badge on his sleeve. Instituted in March 1942, it was awarded for the single-handed destruction of a tank without use of antitank weapons.

▶ A small cemetery is a grim reminder of the reality of war to soldiers moving up to the front in 1943. The traditional markers show those men who were holders of the Iron Cross, while in the background there is one with SS runes.

▼ Panzer Grenadiers cramped in the interior of a SdKfz 251 half track filled with 7.92 mm link for the MG 42 machine gun.

▲ Romanian troops climb aboard an assault gun. Romania eventually withdrew its support for Germany in the spring of 1944 as the Soviet forces were on the border. On August 25, 1944, King Michael declared war on Germany.

The Germans brought 900,000 men, 2,700 tanks and armored vehicles, including the superior Panther and Tiger tanks, the latter armed with a formidable 8.8 cm gun, and 2,000 aircraft to the shoulders of the salient. The attack was first scheduled to begin on May 4 but was cancelled and reinstated for July 5, 1943.

Hitler confessed that he was worried that the operation would not achieve the same level of surprise of previous years. And he was right to be worried. To counter the attack *Stavka*, the Soviet High Command, deployed 20,000 guns, 3,300 tanks, 2,560 aircraft, and 1,337,000 troops. Antitank guns, mines, and infantry bunkers were grouped in armor killing grounds called *Pakfronts*. The minefields were designed to channel the German tanks towards the antitank guns, and if they broke through one layer of defenses there was another behind it. The density of mines was massive, some 2,500 antipersonnel mines, and 2,200 anti-

◀ Dressed in the basic M43 uniform, German soldiers march along a dusty Russian road. The M43 uniform reflected the economies that were being forced on Nazi Germany. It had a high rayon content and was made from shoddy or wool waste.

▲ A PzKpfw IV Ausf F with the short barreled 7.5 cm gun silhouetted at dawn. The attrition of war on the Eastern Front had reduced the panzer divisions from massed formations to *Kampfgruppe*—battle groups, sometimes composed of only a few vehicles.

tank mines per mile of front. In all there were six belts of three to five trench lines about 25 miles deep. Marshal Zhukov planned to break the impetus of the German attack and then he would launch Operations *Kutuzov* and *Rumyantsev*, massive counterattacks to the north and south using men and tanks held in reserve.

So detailed was the Soviet knowledge of the German plan that they launched an artillery bombardment just before the German assault was due to go in. German radar detected the Red Air Force units that were en route to attack and the *Luftwaffe* intercepted the bombers and fighters and so achieved local air superiority.

On the ground the German 9th Army under Field Marshal von Kluge only achieved minor successes against a determined Soviet defense and suffered 25,000 casualties. To the south Field

▲ A *Signal* photograph shows walking wounded making their way back to an aid post in Russia. As casualties mounted the German armed forces began to comb out logistic and administrative units to fill places in the front line.

Marshal von Manstein's 4th *Panzer Armee* made better headway pushing forward 25 miles. On July 12, the 2nd SS-Panzer Corps reached Prokhorovka and encountered the 5th Guards Tank Army that was part of the *Stavka* reserve. In the ensuing maelstrom of dust, smoke, and flame about 1,200 tanks fought the largest tank battle of the war and possibly the largest in history.

The Allied landings on Sicily on July 10 prompted Hitler to order a halt to Operation Citadel. He insisted that the 2nd SS-Panzer Corps, which he rated as the equivalent of 20 Italian divisions, should be withdrawn and sent south to Italy to halt the landings. Two days later Operation *Kutuzov,* the Soviet counterattack in the north by the West Front and Bryansk Front, was launched, and the exhausted German 9th and 2nd Panzer Armies fell back. To the south Operation *Rumyantsev,* the attack by the Voronezh Front and Steppe Front, was launched on August 3. The 4th *Panzer Armee* and Operational Group Kempf fought a hard action as they withdrew, counterattacking and delaying the Soviet advance, but not halting it. By the end of the fighting each

◄ Messerschmitt Bf 109s run up their engines on a wintry air strip in Russia. At the outset of the campaign in the East the *Luftwaffe* was ill-equipped for the extreme temperatures. Oil became viscous and Buna, the artificial rubber developed in Germany, took on the consistency of wood.

▶ A *Waffen-SS* SdKfz 251 in winter camouflage that was part of a *Signal* feature. After the grim experience of the winter of 1941-42, *Waffen-SS* and German soldiers received excellent reversible uniforms for winter warfare. The *Waffen-SS* had a distinctive parka that had a fur trimmed hood.

▼ The soldiers from the half track examine a shot-down Soviet Yakovlev Yak-9. From 1943 onward the Red Air Force received excellent rugged combat aircraft from factories deep in the Urals. The Yak-9 had one 20 mm ShVAK cannon through the propeller hub and one 12.7 Berezin UB machine gun in the upper cowling.

◀ In the *Signal* reportage the men dismount from the half track to attack a village. In winter conditions helmets were not worn routinely because the steel shell was a powerful cold conductor. The parka hoods could also be secured closer to the head of a man wearing a cap.

▶ The 44 tons of a Pz Kpfw V Ausf G Panther proved too much for this Russian timber bridge and it became a recovery problem for its crew.

▲ Among the new weapons deployed by Germans toward the end of the war was the MP 42/StG 44, the world's first assault rifle. It fired a short 7.92 mm round, had a cyclic rate of 500 rpm, and weighed 5.22 kg loaded.

side had lost about 1,500 tanks, but many of the Soviet ones could be recovered and repaired.

Between August and December 1943, the Soviet army in the Ukraine and Belorussia rolled onto an unstoppable offensive. On August 5 Kharkov was finally liberated by the Steppe Front and on September 25 Russian forces recaptured Smolensk. A month later Dneproptrovsk was liberated, and on November 6 Kiev was recaptured by the Voronezh Front. In October, the Kuban bridge-head, was eliminated and this freed the Sea of Azov and gave access to the Black Sea.

The Red Army had always been expert at operations in the winter and so following the autumn muddy season it was back

◄ The *Waffen-SS* troops in the half track have suffered casualties and the *Signal* photograph captures the urgency of stabilizing a wounded man in subzero conditions. Shock combined with extreme cold was as deadly as loss of blood. The man on the right by the stretcher wears the gray wool helmet toque and a *Feldmütze* side cap.

▲ An officer hunches over the handset of a field telephone. Line in contrast to radio equipment was more secure, however German field telephones carried the message *"Achtung Feind hört mit!"* (Warning The Enemy is Listening!).

onto the offensive. On January 19, 1944, the ancient city of Novgorod was liberated. A week later the siege of Leningrad was finally broken as German forces were driven out of artillery range. The city had been almost completely cut off for 900 days and during this time about one million inhabitants had died from disease, starvation, and enemy action.

On March 20 German forces occupied the territory of their wavering Axis partner Hungary to ensure that it remained in the war. On April 2 Soviet forces entered Romanian territory, and on April 25 King Michael of Romania switched allegiances and declared war on Germany. Critically, Germany would no longer have access to the Romanian oil fields at Ploesti and its ships; aircraft and vehicles would be immobilized through lack of fuel.

On the Black Sea the Soviet offensive in the Crimea against the German 17th Army opened on April 8. The Soviet bombardment of Sevastopol was twice as heavy as that employed by the Germans in their attack in 1942, and on May 12, against Hitler's orders, the garrison of 12 German and Romanian divisions surrendered, yielding 25,000 prisoners.

▲ The self-propelled 54 cm mortar Thor, one of the heavy weapons originally developed to smash the Maginot Line. It saw action at Sevastopol and was then deployed in 1944 to pulverize Warsaw. The mortar fired a 1,247 kg shell to a maximum range of 12,500 meters and had a practical rate of fire of four shells an hour. Such impressive weapons were featured in a picture feature in *Signal* as well as on the cover of *Die Wehrmacht*.

To the north, after recapturing territory lost to the USSR in the Winter War of 1939–40, Finland had fought a largely defensive war. In June 1944 with German forces pulling back toward the Reich, a Soviet offensive broke through Finnish defenses and on September 4, 1944, the president, Field Marshal Carl Gustav Mannerheim, signed an armistice with the USSR and declared war on Germany. On September 5 the USSR declared war on Bulgaria, a country that had not fought in Russia, but which was an Axis ally. Two days later Bulgaria declared war on Germany. As the fortunes of war swung against Germany the countries that *Signal* had featured as allies in the battle against Bolshevism became enemies.

On June 22, Operation *Bargration* opened against Army Group Center. Its commander, Field Marshal Ernst Busch, had requested permission to withdraw to stronger positions but was refused by Hitler. In huge armored thrusts the Soviet armored forces encircled and cut off German forces in the Vitebsk, Mogilev, and Bobruysk areas. In four weeks they advanced 450 miles and by July 13 had reached the Polish border. Behind them were 158,000 dead or captured German troops, 2,000 armored vehicles, and 57,000 motor vehicles.

Now *Signal* could only feature stories about individual soldiers with a theme of "Men against Machines"—now the columns of

◄ A machine gun section pauses in the rubble of Warsaw. Two men have fixed chicken wire over their helmets to allow camouflage to be attached. The man on the left has the metal spare barrel container for the MG 42 slung over his shoulder and they all wear an assault order with entrenching tools.

▶ On a side road in Warsaw, soldiers prepare *schweres Wurfgerät* 41, a tubular steel framework for launching 28/32 cm and 30 cm rockets from their crates. Known as the *Stuka zu Fuss*, the sWG 41 was sometimes called the *Heulende Kuh* (Howling Cow).

prisoners and wrecked guns and vehicles in Poland and Belorrusia were German.

On August 1, with Soviet forces advancing the Polish Home Army under General Tadeusz Bor-Komorovski rose to liberate Warsaw. On Stalin's orders, when the Russian forces of the 1st and 2nd Belorussian Fronts reached the River Vistula, they halted. The operational explanation was the need to regroup for the final assault into the Reich. It is also certain that Stalin wanted any potential non-Communist leadership to be destroyed and so he left Warsaw to fight for its life. The battle lasted until October 2 by which time most of the city was in ruins. It was finally

"liberated" by the Russians on January 17, 1945. In January Soviet forces discovered the surviving sick and feeble inmates of the Auschwitz extermination camp. The complex was the most powerful evidence of the Nazi policy of extermination of Jews, Romanies, homosexuals, Poles, Ukrainians, and Soviet prisoners. Over 16 million people were murdered at extermination camps and by *Einsatzgruppen* (Operational Groups) in Russia. It was the fear of Russian revenge for these murderous policies that kept many German soldiers fighting in the East.

To the south the Yugoslav capital of Belgrade had a happier fate than Warsaw, being liberated by Yugoslav and Russian troops on October 20. Three days later the 2nd Belorussian Front entered East Prussia. On Christmas Eve Soviet forces encircled the Hungarian capital of Budapest and after heavy fighting on February 13, it fell.

Eastern Europe's capitals were being captured by Soviet commanders in what seemed like a brutal chess game. On April 13, Vienna was captured. Three days later at 0500 hours, the 1st Belorussian Front under Zhukov began the assault on Berlin. An hour and a half later the 1st Ukrainian Front under Konev swung north to join in the destruction of the capital of the Thousand Year Third Reich.

▲ With several meters of concrete above them a Spanish machine gun crew of the Blue Division look east from the embrasure of a bunker toward the Soviet forces.

▶ *Signal* featured these Spanish soldiers receiving a briefing from their patrol commander in the winter of 1943–44. Franco, Spain's Falangist leader, shrewdly withdrew the Blue Division from Russia when it was obvious that Germany would lose the war. He was the only Fascist leader to remain in power after World War II.

▲ A German patrol slogs through the snow. They wear the two-piece reversible winter uniform with a colored armbands that were regularly changed to ensure front line security.

▶ In this Soviet photograph, an American Dodge Weapons Carrier towing a 20-HM 38 120mm mortar, Russian troops pass the parliament building as they enter Vienna. *Signal* and German propaganda played on the fear of rape and murder by these barbarians from the east.

NORMANDY AND EUROPE

"For the last time our deadly enemies the Jewish Bolsheviks have launched their massive forces to the attack. Their aim is to reduce Germany to ruins and to exterminate our people. Form yourselves into a sworn brotherhood, to defend, not the empty conception of a Fatherland, but your homes, your wives, your children, and, with them, our future."

—Adolf Hitler *Order of the Day, April 15, 1945.*

This Spanish language *Signal* cover focuses on the production battle in Germany. He III bombers, medium artillery and the production line of some of the 418 *Panzerjäger* 38 (t) Marder III 7.5 cm self-propelled antitank guns built between 1942–43 are featured in the magazine.

I N THE AUTUMN OF 1944, Dr. Joseph Goebbels, one of the orig-inators of *Signal*, was designated *Generallbevollmächtigter für den totalen Kriegeinsatz* (General Plenipotentiary for the Total War Effort). To keep Germany at war, he used the brutal "stick" of imprisonment and execution, even for relatives, with the "carrot" of the promise of victory through Wonder Weapons.

Now *Signal* had no victories to report but concentrated on pictures of armaments production and youthful antiaircraft crews and workers. Women had been drafted into the factories and one *Signal* cover showed a youngster checking the engine of a Bf 109 fighter on the production line.

The most famous of the Wonder Weapons trumpeted by Goebbels were the two long-range missiles the Fieseler FZG 76 and the Peenemünde A-4. They were named *Vergeltungswaffe* or Revenge Weapons by Hitler and became the V1 and V2. The V1 was a winged missile. Effectively the first cruise missile powered by a pulse jet engine, it had a characteristic popping or buzzing sound in flight. In England it was nicknamed the "Doodlebug" or "Buzz Bomb." The V2 was a far more sophisticated missile with

▲ A chemist conducts a test. By 1945 women were playing a vital role in research and production for the German war effort as this 1944 *Signal* cover illustrates. As the war swung against Germany the magazine struggled to find positive images and so concentrated on the home front.

(ABOVE) One of the camouflaged Me 262 assembly lines in a pine forest near Augsburg and (RIGHT) the Heinkel He 162 *Volksjäger* "People's Fighter." This stop-gap aircraft used non-strategic materials in a desperate attempt to regain air superiority.

▲ Gunners with a coastal battery, visible in the background, pass through the gates of the barbed wire perimeter.

◄ Men of the garrison of an Atlantic Wall strong point run to their positions behind a camouflaged reinforced concrete antitank wall.

a liquid fuel engine, fin stabilization, and a pre-set guidance system.

The V1 had a maximum speed of 560 kph, range of 260 km, and a warhead of 850 kg of HE. Some 8,900 were launched against Britain, the first landing on June 13, and another 12,000 were aimed elsewhere in Europe, notably Antwerp. The V2 had a maximum speed of 610 kph, range of 305 km, and a 1,000 kg warhead. Production began in early 1944 and about 10,000 were made, of which 1,115 were fired against Britain, the first landing on September 8, and 1,535 against other targets.

V1 launch sites were under construction in France before D Day and with pictures of the concrete coastal defenses and artillery batteries of the Atlantic Wall, *Signal* fostered an illusion that North West Europe was safe from invasion—it was *Festung Europa* (Fortress Europe). For many of the Germans garrisoned in France, Belgium, and the Netherlands, the posting was a rest from the rigors of the Eastern Front.

▲ A 40.6 cm SK C/34 gun of *Batterie Lindemann* emplaced near Cap Griz Nez. The guns had an elevation of 60° and could fire a 1,030 kg shell to a range of 56,000 meters. They had been intended for the proposed "H" Class of battleship and were installed either singly or in pairs in reinforced concrete fortifications.

◀ *Signal* featured these British photographs of Commandos in training. Amphibious and Commando raids reached their violent climax with Dieppe on August 18–19, 1942, when the German defenders stopped Canadian forces almost on the shoreline.

▲ A machine gunner brings his MG 34 into position in a Tobruk Stand, a one or two man reinforced concrete bunker, on the Atlantic Wall. The bunkers and trenches covered the coastal minefields, (above right). Reliable and well constructed German antitank (AT), antipersonnel (AP) mines and cruelly ingenious booby traps would cause considerable losses throughout the war. After D Day they would delay but not halt the eastward drive by the Allies.

From as early as 1940 British Commandos had raided the coast, but the German garrison had also enjoyed distinct victories. On February 12, 1942, the battle cruisers KMS *Gneisenau* and KMS *Scharnhorst,* and the heavy cruiser KMS *Prinz Eugen* sailed from Brest in France to the security of the Elbe River in Germany. Operation *Cerberus* known to the British as the "Channel Dash" was celebrated by *Signal*.

Later that year on August 18–19, an Anglo-Canadian force raided the French coastal town of Dieppe. It was a disaster—out of a force of 5,000 the Canadians lost 3,379 killed or captured. *Signal* published photographs of wrecked Churchill tanks on the beach and the shocked and wounded prisoners.

The U-boat campaign against Allied merchant shipping in the North Atlantic was fought from the French naval bases in Brittany, Normandy, and the Biscay seaboard. *Signal* featured the U-boats and their crews and the cramped and dangerous world they inhabited. The U-boat campaign could have destroyed the United Kingdom except that ULTRA intercepts allowed convoys to be routed around the Wolf Packs of U-boats and helped escorts locate and attack the submarines.

On the night of May 30, 1942, the Allied bombing campaign against Germany and targets in Occupied Europe changed forever when the RAF under Air Marshal Arthur Harris launched the Thousand-Bomber Raid on Cologne. On July 24, 1943, in Operation *Gomorrah*, the RAF attacked Hamburg and in the firestorm that followed 50,000 people were killed. At night the RAF attacked the Ruhr, Berlin, and industrial and political targets. The USAAF 8th Air Force concentrated on daylight raids against high value military and industrial targets. For *Signal* it was hard to disguise the constant battering by the Allies so it concentrated on the civilian casualties and destruction of historic buildings by "terror flyers."

The young *Luftwaffe* fighter pilots were the new heroes to be celebrated by *Signal*. In 1945 they became the pioneers of future aerial combat when they piloted the Messerschmitt Me-262 *Schwalbe* (Swallow) jet fighter. Earlier in July 1944, the Messerschmitt Me-163 *Komet* (Comet) went into action against USAAF B-17s. It was powered by a liquid fueled rocket motor that gave a duration of ten minutes. The aircraft took off on a wheeled dolly and landed on a skid which could be fatal if there were fuel residues in the aircraft's tanks. The Me-163 was 5.7 meters long and had a wingspan of 9.3 m. Its Walter rocket motor developed 1700 kg static thrust and a climb rate of 10,000 meters in 2.6 seconds. It was armed with two 30-mm cannon and had a top speed of 959 kilometers per hour.

The Me 262, a single-seat fighter, was powered by two 109-004B1 Jumo turbojets and had a maximum speed of 539 mph (868 km/h). Armed with four 30-mm cannon it could also mount the 5.5-cm R4M unguided air-to-air missile. This consisted of a steel tube with solid fuel motor and eight spring-loaded fins that deployed after it had been launched. The warhead was 500 grams of HE and at launch the missile accelerated to 550 meters a second.

In the last few weeks of the war six Me 262s, each armed with two banks of 24 R4Ms, took off against a formation of USAAF B-17E Flying Fortresses on a daylight raid. In minutes they had shot down fourteen bombers and with no losses returned to base.

By the summer of 1944, the manpower shortage in Germany had become so severe that military units in France contained former POWs from the Eastern Front. Men with hearing and intestinal problems formed a "Stomach and Ear Battalions."

▶ The U-boat war waged from bases along the French Atlantic coast put Britain under considerable pressure. At the beginning of the war the Wolf Pack tactics that concentrated submarines against convoys could be lethally effective. *Signal* celebrated the U-boat aces and the crews who ventured out into the Atlantic on long and increasingly hazardous patrols.

▶ *Signal* gleefully printed this cover picture of Churchill to reinforce the propaganda that, unlike Germany with its clean living *Führer*, Britain was led by a self-indulgent drunkard.

▲ *Signal* employed graphic artists, whose dramatic images illustrated facets of the war that could not be covered by photographers. Here an Me 110 night fighter shoots down a representational RAF bomber.

▶ An RAF Avro Lancaster shot down by Flak or night fighters burns out. With a crew of seven and a range of 4,070 km, it was capable of carrying 8,165 kg of bombs.

For the British and American planners in Britain the site for the invasion of Europe, or Second Front, was constrained by the range at which fighter aircraft could operate from Britain, suitable beaches for landing large numbers of troops, and weather, tidal, and moon states. The German staff at Field Marshal von Rundstedt's HQ in France looked at the logical options and decided that the Boulogne-Calais area was the most likely site for an invasion. Allied deception plans, code named Bodyguard, helped to foster this impression and ULTRA intercepts confirmed that the Germans had taken the bait.

◀ An American photographer captures the nervous anticipation in U.S. soldiers in a follow wave at Omaha Beach in Normandy in June 1944 as they wait behind the ramp of a Landing Craft Tank (LCT) nosing toward the beach. Following the success of the Allied invasion the *Signal* editorial team that had been based in Paris since 1940 closed their office and moved back to Germany.

▲ A captured German photograph shows American paratroopers wounded in fighting in Normandy receiving first aid from a German corporal in a front-line position.

The Allied landings on the Normandy coast on June 6, 1944, were codenamed Operation *Overlord*. There were five beaches from west to east. The U.S. Army landed at Utah and Omaha, the British and Canadians at Gold, Juno, and Sword. Landings by paratroops and airborne forces of the British 6th Airborne Division secured the west flank and the U.S. 82nd and 101st Airborne Divisions secured the approaches to Utah where the U.S. VIII Corps landed with minimal casualties. Only at Omaha were there significant losses where the U.S. 1st Infantry Division, part of the U.S. V Corps was faced by the fresh German 352nd Infantry Division. The "Big Red One" suffered 2,000 casualties on the beach before it gained a foothold. By midnight on June 6, 57,000 American troops and 75,000 British and Canadian were ashore. Allied casualties were 2,500 killed and 8,500 wounded. The USAAF and RAF had flown 14,000 sorties and lost 127 aircraft.

Once ashore the Allies fought a tough campaign in the Normandy fields or *Bocage*. On July 18, the U.S. 1st Army broke out of the beachhead at St Lô fighting through the 2nd SS-Panzer Division. Two days later the Bomb Plot against Hitler by liberal and Christian German officers failed, when a device exploded at Hitler's HQ, the *Wolfsschanze* (The Wolf's Lair) in Rastenburg, East Prussia, but failed to kill him.

By August 21 the American breakout and Anglo-Canadian attack towards Caen trapped the German 5th *Panzer Armee*, 7th

▸ A heavily camouflaged patrol of youthful Grenadiers of the *Waffen-SS* Division "*Hitlerjugend*," have landmarks indicated before they go forward in July 1944. Formed in June 1943, with an average age of 18, the division fought with particular ferocity in Normandy.

▾ A grim faced machine gunner of the *Waffen-SS*. Belief in final victory was being replaced by a hope of a split between the Allies and sustained by reports of powerful "wonder weapons".

Army, and Panzer Group Eberbach, and their equipment in the Argentan-Falaise pocket. Some 10,000 Germans were killed and 50,000 surrendered. Over 560 tanks, nearly a thousand artillery pieces, and 7,500 motor vehicles were abandoned. On August 25, French troops entered Paris. The Allies raced eastward and on September 3, Brussels was liberated and a day later Antwerp.

The dramatic and ill-conceived Operation *Market-Garden* that used airborne forces to seize bridges over the lower Rhine and outflank the German Westwall defenses was launched on September 17. The 82nd and 101st Airborne Divisions captured their objectives, but the British at Arnhem were counterattacked and eventually Montgomery was forced to order a withdrawal on September 25. The British lost 1,130 killed and 6,000 taken prisoner. The Germans suffered 3,300 casualties.

▴ *Signal* published this picture of Allied troop-carrying gliders on a landing zone in Holland with the implication that they were downed aircraft. The Allies quickly recovered from disaster at Arnhem.

▲ An Allied photograph of captured German infantry waiting to be processed before being transported to the rear.

◄ With an abandoned U.S. Army M8 armored car on the road behind them, German soldiers enjoy good Virginia tobacco. The man on the left holds a captured M1911A1 Colt 45 pistol. The men's entrenching tools have been positioned so that the blade protects their heart—as in World War 1.

▶ The crew of a *Waffen-SS* 4 x 41 Pkw Typ K2s/Typ 166 VW *Schwimmwagen,* the amphibious reconnaissance vehicle built by Volkswagen, check their way during the Ardennes offensive in December 1944.

◄ An American army combat photographer captures the moment as airborne soldiers move off from their Waco CG-4A troop-carrying gliders following the Rhine crossing on March 23, 1945. The Waco could carry 17,256 kg of stores like a Jeep or an M1A1 75-mm pack howitzer, or 13 troops.

On December 16, 1944, despite indicators through ULTRA intercepts, the Allies were taken by surprise when Hitler launched *Unternehmen Wacht am Rhein* (Operation Watch on the Rhine) in the quiet Ardennes sector. Three armies were employed—5th Panzer, 6th *SS-Panzer Armee,* and 7th Panzer. They broke through and created a salient in the front held by the U.S. 1st Army and the 12th Army Group. The heroic defense of Bastogne by the 101st Airborne slowed the German attack. A combination of lack of fuel and improved weather that allowed the Allied airforces to operate in a ground attack role halted the offensive. It had cost the Allies 77,000 casualties but the Germans had suffered 130,000 and lost valuable guns and vehicles.

The fight for Germany was now in the hands of the fanatical and the very young and very old. *Waffen-SS* troops and *Fallschirmjäger* at times found themselves fighting alongside the *Volkssturm* (literally the Peoples' Storm), the German civilian home defense force established in September 1944 and composed of civilian males between 16 and 60 who were capable of bearing arms. It was trained and organized on military lines, but a shortage of weapons restricted both training and operational deployment. In January 1945, Hitler ordered that the *Volkssturm* be amalgamated with regular army units which accounted for the number of schoolboys and older men taken prisoners by the Allies at the end of the war.

▲ In street fighting in Germany a GI armed with the M1 Garand self-loading rifle surveys the remains of a burned-out building in a photograph posed for an Allied photographer. Only as ground troops entered the Third Reich were the Allies made fully aware of the massive level of destruction caused by air raids.

▲ In this French army photograph a patrol of *Goumiers*, French colonial troops from North Africa, pass a grotesque figure created from a bronze bust of Hitler and a shop window manikin.

▲ Hanna Reitsch shows her Iron Cross First Class to her mother. She received the decoration in 1942 for her work as a test pilot that included flying a piloted VI.

On February 9, 1945, the Allies reached the Rhine and, on March 7, the U.S. 87th Division captured intact the Ludendorff railway bridge that spanned the river at Remagen. On March 23 in Operation Varsity, a major set piece operation, the Allies crossed the Rhine at Rees. The Ruhr, the industrial heartland of Germany, was surrounded by the U.S. 1st and 9th Armies and the huge pocket fell on April 18. On April 13 the Allies liberated Belsen and Buchenwald concentration camps, and on April 25 they liberated Dachau.

The nemesis of the Third Reich was reaching its violent conclusion further west as the pincers of the Red Army closed in on Berlin. The Soviet offensive began on April 16 with huge pincers driving past the city and surrounding it by the 25th. The city, already badly damaged by RAF raids, was fought for street by street from the suburbs to the Reichstag in the center. Hitler was now living a troglodyte life in the *Führerbunker,* the two story concrete bunker by the Reich Chancellery. He continued issuing orders to armies that no longer existed. On April 20 Hitler celebrated his 56th birthday, and among his visitors was the pioneering aviatrix Hanna Reitsch, who evaded Soviet fighters and AA fire and landed in parkland near the bunker.

On April 30 Soviet troops raced into the ruined Reichstag, climbed to the top and raised their flag. On the same day Hitler shot himself after giving instructions that his body should be burned.

On May 2 General Karl Weidling, the commandant of the Berlin garrison, instructed it to surrender and about 136,000 men went into captivity. In the ruins were the bodies of over 100,000 civil-

◀ In this Allied photograph an honor guard presents arms at the grave of some of the dead at Vaihingen Concentration Camp. Sights like this shocked the Allied soldiers.

▶ A French Army 75 mm M10 Tank Destroyer enters Stuttgart on the German border. Rubble from bomb damage was stacked against buildings to protect them and keep streets clear.

▲ In the winter of 1945 German soldiers plod across a town square in Ostheim into captivity—the Allied photographic censor has painted out the place name from the inn sign behind them.

ians who had died in the fighting, about the same number of Soviet soldiers who had been killed in the battle for Berlin.

For Germany their war was over, it had cost the lives of 4,500,000 servicemen and women and that of 2,000,000 civilians. Poland had grabbed areas of East Prussia and the port of Danzig as the Soviet Union had encroached on Poland's eastern borders and refugees had fled west, producing a net population movement of 9,500,000 between 1939 and 1947. For administrative purposes Germany was divided into French, American, British, and Russian zones and the national capital in the Russian zone was split four ways.

The country and city would remain divided until 1989—fifty years after the beginning of World War II.

▲ The war ends in Berlin. With a World War I tank brought out from a museum for the final battle, and the Bellevue Palace and the Lustgarten in the background, two Russian soldiers pose for an Allied photographer as armed tourists in the capital of the Third Reich.

INDEX